THE GAMBLE HOUSE
COOKBOOK
GOOD DESIGN | GOOD FOOD

THE GAMBLE HOUSE
COOKBOOK
GOOD DESIGN | GOOD FOOD

Introduction by Edward R. Bosley
Foreword and Selected Recipes by Mark Peel
Photography by Meg McComb, Tim Street-Porter, and Alex Vertikoff
Edited by Barbara Harris Cury

Balcony Press

DAVID GAMBLE   MARY GAMBLE

TABLE OF CONTENTS

DEDICATION

To The Gamble House docents past, present, and future. Your generosity and enthusiasm make visitors feel at home in "our house." Your spirit provides joy for all of us at The Gamble House.

Published in the United States of America in 2008 by Balcony Press.
No part of this book may be reproduced in any manner without written permission except in the case of brief quotations embodied in critical articles and reviews.
For information, address Balcony Media, Inc., 512 E. Wilson Avenue, Suite 213, Glendale California 91206.

The Cookbook Committee
Editor-in-Chief Barbara Harris Cury
Associate Editor Elizabeth Harris
John Azar, Janet Boyer, Jan Horner, Pat Lem, Joann Lynch, Millie E. Rodstrom, Cleo Rogers, Maria Tornek, Sylvia Watson

Book Design | Leslie Baker Graphic Design
Printing and Production | Navigator Cross-media
Printed in South Korea

Photographs © 2008 by Meg McComb, Tim Street-Porter, and Alex Vertikoff

Library of Congress Control Number: 2008927007
ISBN 978-1-890449-48-3

CHARLES SUMNER GREEENE   HENRY MATHER GREEENE

Left to right: Margaret Gamble Messler Winslow, Joseph D. Messler, Jr., Tracy Gamble Hirrel, circa 1952

"We all fed the goldfish. I am certain they looked forward to Sundays because they knew that the eating was going to be easy! Those fish must have eaten 10 pounds of food on the days we were there."

—JOSEPH D. MESSLER, JR.

THE GAMBLE HOUSE

In 1908, Mary and David Gamble built a winter home in Pasadena designed by Charles and Henry Greene. The classic California bungalow design planned with meticulous attention to every detail of the home is an icon of the American Arts and Crafts movement and a National Historic Landmark. This American treasure attracts thousands of visitors from around the world every year. Today, via television, internet, and print media, more and more people are introduced to or reacquainted with the craftsmanship, functionality, and beauty of the Gambles' Pasadena home. The Gamble House one hundred years later remains virtually unchanged from 1909 when Mary and David Gamble began wintering at 4 Westmoreland Place.

After World War II, Cecil Gamble, the oldest son of Mary and David Gamble, moved into the house with his wife Louise. Following his death, the heirs of Louise and Cecil Gamble presented the Gamble House as a gift in 1966 to the City of Pasadena in a joint agreement with the School of Architecture at the University of Southern California.

In 1967, the Docent Council was formed to welcome the public to the house, giving personal, individualized, and fact-filled tours to impart an understanding of the Craftsman style. Docent Council members also volunteer time at The Gamble House Bookstore, the Greene and Greene Archives and exhibition at the Huntington Library in San Marino. They train selected middle school students to become junior docents.

Each year Gamble House visitors come to learn about the architecture and furnishings designed by the Greenes. What they cannot appreciate, however, is the quality of the family experiences enjoyed by the Gambles in their home, including the meals that were served.

We are privileged to present in this cookbook a few recipes written by Mary Gamble and served at the elegant San Domingo mahogany and ebony dining table in the dining room. These recipes were shared with us by some of the great-grandchildren of David and Mary Gamble.

The majority of recipes in this centennial collection, however, are dishes created by dedicated members of the Docent Council of The Gamble House, volunteers who truly make the house a living, breathing home, however temporary, to our visitors. Early in the Docent Council history, docents began inviting friends and prospective volunteers to monthly luncheons for which they prepared and served favorite recipes. These memorable times became an enduring tradition in which friendships were enhanced and a passion for the Gamble House was further inspired. In 1972, docents first published a collection of favorite recipes served at these events. Two more books with new recipes followed, one in 1979 and one in 1987. In honor of The Gamble House's centennial year, the docents have created a new cookbook.

Many of these recipes have been served at Gamble House social events; others are graciously shared as personal favorites. All have been selected for your enjoyment and for you to feel in some way closer to life at 4 Westmoreland Place.

EDWARD R. BOSLEY | James N. Gamble Director | The Gamble House

Top Row (left to right): Elizabeth Gamble Messler, Joseph Dicus Messler, M.D., Margaret Gamble Swift, James N. Gamble, Harriet Gamble, Mary Corinne Gamble Ritchey
Bottom Row: Betsy Swift Mitchell, Anne Swift Lord, Joseph D. Messler, Jr., Margaret Gamble Messler Winslow, Tracy Gamble Hirrel, circa 1956

"We sat through hours of photo sessions in the living room. Our uncle, Jim Gamble, arranged his lights and camera and posed us in front of the inglenook fireplace. Almost always the resulting snapshots showed parents struggling to hang on to squirming children who had clothing askew, panties showing, or impatient children captured candidly on camera."

—JOSEPH D. MESSLER, JR.

THE KITCHEN

Greene and Greene designed the kitchen, butler's pantry, and cold room as integrated working spaces for the use of the Gambles' staff. Although the Gamble family may not have been especially familiar with this functional and seemingly plain side of the house, the kitchen area benefits from the same attention to detail as the rest of the house. The lighter color of the maple cabinets and sugar pine counter tops would have looked startlingly different from the fine finishes and dark paneling of the public spaces, but they were selected for the practicality of kitchen use. Superbly designed cabinets, well-proportioned spaces for ease of movement when cooking, and beautifully made objects such as the island table with drawers that open from either side for equal ease are notable features here. Double-hung sash windows allow cooking odors to exit without having large casement window panels swing into the work space. Linoleum, an 1860s British innovation made from flax, linseed oil and ground cork dust, originally covered the maple sub-flooring for durability and ease of cleaning. In 1908, it was a modern material for a modern work space. Linoleum is scheduled to return to The Gamble House as one of the interior restoration initiatives recommended by the Historic Structures Report.

EDWARD R. BOSLEY | James N. Gamble Director | The Gamble House

THE ROOM FOR DINING

The Gamble House dining room wraps itself around those who are gathered there. Its simple geometry and its magnificent art glass chandelier center attention on the table and encourage those present to feel close. Its walls and cabinets, all its furnishings, capture our attention inside. That the entire surround is so beautifully crafted, using materials of intrinsic quality and interest, sustains our attention and rewards repeated visits.

Great architects seem to know that houses are only partly about capturing a view or, in southern California, connecting inside and outside. Houses exist because we need the rooms that accommodate everyday life and special occasions. Greene and Greene designed the Gamble House dining room as a place for being together. Its windows allow light of varying intensity and color to animate the room as the day passes and as the seasons change. Twin doors allow passage to and from an adjacent terrace. But these are not the windows and doors that bond inside and outside. Rather, their character is more an open net through which views are caught. Walking from the great entrance hall to the dining room is a memorable experience. The transition from the dining room out to the terrace is not seamless — it is an event to be felt and enjoyed. To be in the dining room is a privilege the family shared every day. To be in such a room as a guest must have seemed like an honor. To visit the room now is simply a joy.

ROBERT S. HARRIS, FAIA | Emeritus Professor of Architecture
University of Southern California

Left to right: Margaret Gamble Messler Winslow, Elizabeth Gamble Messler, Joseph Dicus Messler, M.D., Joseph D. Messler, Jr., circa 1953

"Some of us remember trying to get through the front door as quickly as possible to escape the clutches of my grandfather, Cecil, whom we called "Bonty". He greeted us with a swat on our behinds accompanied by a shout of "Whammy!" It was a welcome that truly traumatized my oldest cousin, Louise, who still talks about it to this day."

—JOSEPH D. MESSLER, JR.

THE FAMILY COOK

In 1911, Mary Gamble wrote the recipes that appear in this book presumably for her cook. Although 1911 may not seem that long ago, in culinary terms one hundred years is light years away. Striking to me are both the types of dishes that were being prepared in the Gamble household and the shorthand manner in which the recipes were written. In their original form, these recipes, that would have been easy for Mrs. Gamble's staff to decipher, are practically unusable for the contemporary cook.

Kitchen equipment, too, has changed since the early 20th century and would not be used by today's cook. For example, in Mrs. Gamble's day, a popular item was the spider — a heavy frying pan with legs that sat above the flame.

One hundred years ago, any family of substance, even with a moderate income, had servants and cooks. They were not "personal assistants" or "private chefs" but typical servants and cooks who knew their métiers well. Cooks were expected to know how to prepare a standard repertoire of dishes, which by today's standards would be quite broad. Organ meats and variety meats were widely consumed—and with great relish. Game was still common. However, fresh fruits and vegetables were difficult to obtain outside of their local peak seasons.

The original recipes you see here are not really recipes, as we know them, but notes for already accomplished cooks who had been with the family for years. The food is simple and flavorful, with no regard for calories or saturated fats. All of the ingredients in Mrs. Gamble's recipes shown here are available any time of the year. These recipes give us a window on an era that is definitely gone, but not so long gone. The flavors would be familiar to all of us, and many of the dishes would be as well—if we could just figure out exactly how they were made.

MARK PEEL | Proprietor and Executive Chef | Campanile Restaurant, Los Angeles

Almond Pudding.

1 pt. shelled almonds. 2 doz. macaroons. the grated rind of a lemon. half a cupful of sugar. half a cupful of butter. the yolk of 6 eggs. 1 qt. milk. 1 pt. cream. one tablespoonful rice flour. Blanch the almonds and pound them in a mortar. Put the milk in a double boiler. reserving half a cupful. Add the pounded almonds to it; mix the rice flour with the half cupful of cold milk and stir into the boiling milk. Cook six minutes and put away to cool. When about half cooled add the sugar and butter, which should have been beaten together until light. When cold add the yolks of the eggs well beaten. the macaroons, which have been dried and rolled fine, and the cream. Butter a pudding dish which will hold a little more than two quarts, or two small ones will do. Turn the mixture into this, and bake slowly 45 minutes, serve cold. Half this quantity will make a good sized pudding.

ALMOND PUDDING

Today we would call this a custard or flan. The amaretto macaroons are important because they are made with bitter almonds or sometimes with the kernels from apricot pits. This adds a refreshing bitter edge to the flavor. Making this is well worth the effort.

....

2 cups milk
1 ½ teaspoons rice flour
12 stale amaretto macaroons
1 cup blanched almonds finely ground in a food processor fitted with a steel blade,
    or 1 cup almond meal
Zest of ½ lemon, finely chopped
½ cup sugar
4 tablespoons (½ stick) unsalted butter, at room temperature, plus more
    for greasing pan
3 egg yolks
1 cup heavy cream

Measure out ¼ cup of the milk and dissolve the rice flour in it. Set aside.

If the macaroons are not stale, allow them to dry out in a low oven (200°) for 20 minutes. Place in a food processor fitted with a steel blade and pulse to a fine meal. Add the almond meal and lemon zest and pulse together.

Beat together the sugar and butter until fluffy. Set aside.

Preheat oven to 325°.

Grease a 1-quart soufflé or pudding dish.

Place the remaining milk in a heavy saucepan or in the top of a double boiler and bring to a boil over medium heat. Stir in the almond meal mixture and reduce heat to medium low. Stirring constantly, add the milk and rice flour mixture and cook, stirring, for 6 minutes. Remove from heat. Cool to lukewarm.

Stir the butter and sugar into the milk mixture. Cool to room temperature. Beat in the egg yolks, one at a time, and the cream.

Pour mixture into the prepared dish. Place in a larger baking pan and add enough boiling water to the pan to come halfway up the sides of the soufflé dish. Bake 40 – 50 minutes in the water bath until firm but still slightly quivery in the center when gently shaken. Remove from the heat, allow to cool, then cover and chill. Serve cold.

Serves 6–8

SAVORY CHESTNUT PUDDING

This dense pudding is really a savory custard, and it makes a tasty side dish for a fall or winter holiday meal. The butter was reduced by half to prevent the pudding from separating. To serve it as a dessert, triple the sugar.

....

Butter or oil for greasing
1 pound chestnuts or 12 to14 ounces vacuum-packed chestnuts
1½ cups milk
6 eggs, beaten
6 tablespoons unsalted butter, softened
Pinch of salt
2 tablespoons light brown sugar, tightly packed
½ teaspoon vanilla extract

Preheat oven to 350°. Lightly butter a 1-quart soufflé dish or pudding dish.

Bring a large pot of water to a boil. Meanwhile, use a paring knife to cut an "x" on the flat side of each chestnut. Drop the chestnuts into the boiling water and boil for 5 minutes. Remove a chestnut, run under cold water to cool, and peel off the shell and inner brown skin. If the chestnut does not peel easily, boil for another few minutes. Turn off the heat, and, one by one, remove a chestnut, run under cold water and remove the peels and skins. If using vacuum-packed chestnuts, omit this step.

Place the chestnuts on a baking sheet and roast until thoroughly dry and toasty, about 30 minutes. Remove and cool. Transfer chestnuts to a food processor fitted with a steel blade and process to a fine meal.

Whisk together the milk and eggs in a large bowl. Beat the butter, salt, and sugar together in a stand mixer fitted with the paddle attachment, or with a hand mixer, until fluffy. Add the chestnuts to the mixture and beat well. Add the milk, eggs, and vanilla. Combine thoroughly.

Pour into the buttered soufflé dish. Place in a larger baking pan and add enough boiling water to the baking pan to come halfway up the sides of the soufflé dish. Bake 45–60 minutes in the water bath in the oven until firm but still slightly quivery in the center when gently shaken. Serve immediately or at room temperature.

Note: For a more savory pudding, lightly sauté ¼ cup minced celery and 1 tablespoon minced shallots until soft in 1 tablespoon butter. Add ¼ teaspoon salt and ¼–½ teaspoon fresh ground pepper, or more to taste. Add to the chestnut mixture. Serve with a sherry wine sauce if you desire.

For a dessert pudding, use 6 tablespoons brown sugar. Serve pudding dusted with confectioners sugar and whipped cream or vanilla ice cream.

Serves 6–8

Chestnut Pudding

Boil a quantity of chestnuts, first slitting
the skins of each with a sharp knife to
prevent their bursting When they become
tender take them out of their skins and put
the meats into an oven. When they are
thoroughly dry pulverize them, and then
make a batter as follows. 6 ounces of good
butter, beat it to a cream, and then add
8 ounces powdered chestnuts, 2 tablespoons
sifted loaf sugar, a few drops of vanilla
extract, 3/4 of a pint of milk and 6 whisked
eggs. Beat the mixture well together
pour it into a buttered mold, cover the top
with buttered paper and bake in a good oven
Send it to the table with wine sauce

Clove Cake

1 pound flour   1 pound sugar
1   "   seeded raisins   3/4 "   butter
1 cup thin sour cream. 4 eggs.
1 nutmeg; peel of 1 lemon grated.
1 tablespoonful ground cloves
1 glass brandy or wine.
1 teaspoon saleratus dissolved in water
or milk.
1 cup English Walnuts chopped fine.
Put some whole nut meats on top of frosting.

Fruit Jumbles.

1 cup butter.   1 cup sugar
2½   "   flour.   ½ "   sweet milk
3 eggs   ½ nutmeg grated.
3 teaspoons baking powder.
1 cup currants.
Spread on a broad shallow tin
the thickness of cookies.
Cut in squares while warm.

FRUIT JUMBLES

The original recipe has no instructions because it was assumed, no doubt, that the cook knew what to do. Judging from the ingredients, the batter is put together like a pound cake or brownies. I reduced the "one half a nutmeg" in Mrs. Gamble's recipe—which measured to be nearly 2 teaspoons nutmeg to a much more reasonable amount that, nonetheless, results in a sweet, spicy cake, perfect with a cup of tea. Just before serving, you may want to sprinkle the cake with powdered sugar.

1 cup currants
½ cup white wine
1 cup water
Oil for greasing pan
2 ½ cups all-purpose flour
½ teaspoon freshly grated nutmeg
1 tablespoon baking powder
½ pound (2 sticks) butter, at room temperature
1 cup sugar
3 eggs
½ cup sweetened condensed milk

Place currants in a bowl. Combine the wine and water in a small saucepan and bring it to a boil. Pour over the currants and let sit for 10 minutes. Drain and dry the currants on paper towels or a clean dishtowel.

Preheat oven to 350°. Oil a 9" x 12" baking pan and line with parchment paper. Oil the parchment paper. Sift together the flour, nutmeg, and baking powder.

In a standing mixer fitted with the paddle attachment, beat together the butter and sugar at medium speed until fluffy, about 2 minutes. Add the eggs, one at a time, scraping down the bowl after each addition.

Add the flour mixture in 3 parts, alternating with the condensed milk, and ending with flour. Stir in the currants.

Spread evenly in the prepared pan and bake 30 minutes or until the cake pulls away from the sides of the pan and a tester comes out clean. Allow to cool in the pan for 10 minutes, then reverse onto a rack and allow to cool. If you don't plan to serve immediately, cut the cake into squares and wrap tightly in plastic wrap and foil.

Serves 16

Calf's Liver Patties.

Chop the liver fine, scrape salt pork
mix with it fine herbs, bay leaves,
pepper, salt and two eggs. Line a brown
bread tin with strips of salt pork, By
buttering the tin you can make it stay
in place; Mix the eggs with it, set it
in a pan of hot water, cover and bake
for 2½ hours.

Sweet Bread Havanese.

Fry the sweet bread, without blanching,
in butter so they will be evenly browned,
serve with a tomato sauce, with plenty
of fresh red peppers chopped and mixed
with it. Take green peppers about two
or three inches long, stuff with mushrooms, truffles, a little bread crumbs
cook in the sauce. Bake or broil, serve
with it.
     The skins can be taken off by placing
the peppers in the oven, then peel the
skins off before filling

SWEETBREADS HAVANESE

"Havanese" must refer to the peppers. A stuffed red pepper such as a small pimento pepper would be better than a green pepper because it cooks faster and is a more appropriate portion size. Cooking sweetbreads without the traditional blanching as Mrs. Gamble indicates is, in fact, faster and easier without any change in texture or taste.

1 ½ pounds sweetbreads, soaked in ice water for one hour
5 small fresh pimento peppers
6 tablespoons olive oil
3/4 cup finely diced onion, divided in half
1 tablespoon minced garlic
1 ½ cups prepared tomato sauce
½ pound mushrooms, wiped
Salt, pepper
¼ cup breadcrumbs
¾ cup flour
2 tablespoons butter

Blacken peppers on all sides over a flame or under a broiler. Place them in a plastic bag and let cool for 5 minutes, then peel the skin. Slice and reserve the tops of the peppers. Remove the seeds and ribs. Finely dice one pepper. Place the remaining peppers aside.

Heat 2 tablespoons of the olive oil over medium heat and sauté the diced pepper, ½ of the onion, and the garlic until soft but not browned. Add tomato sauce and ½ cup water; simmer gently 20 minutes, stirring occasionally. Season with salt and pepper.

While the sauce simmers, preheat oven to 350°.

Coarsely chop the mushrooms. Heat 2 tablespoons of oil over medium heat and sauté mushrooms and remaining onions until soft. Season with salt and pepper and cook until mushroom liquid evaporates. Stir in breadcrumbs. Stuff the 4 peppers with mushroom mixture and replace top. Place peppers in a shallow baking dish. Pour the tomato sauce around them and bake 20 minutes, uncovered.

Pat the sweetbreads dry, season them with salt and pepper and dredge them in flour. Heat 2 tablespoons oil with the butter in a heavy skillet over medium-high heat. Reduce heat to medium and sauté the sweetbreads until browned on both sides, about 4 minutes per side. Slice into 1" thick pieces and serve with baked peppers and sauce.

Serves 4

PECAN CAKE

Mary Gamble's recipe for pecan cake is a confusing one for the contemporary reader/
cook and clearly illustrates that Mrs. Gamble was writing these for her cooks, whom she
(or somebody else) had trained. The recipe looks as if she might want the icing to be
a royal icing or fondant, since she calls for powdered sugar and talks about adding the
pineapple and pecans while the icing is still soft. But a royal icing calling for six egg whites
would take a ton of powdered sugar (six cups), which doesn't make a lot of sense,
especially if the icing is going to be used to fill the layer cake, too. So I've made the icing a
meringue. Despite the number of egg whites, the cake is dense and very delicious.

For the cake:

Oil for pans
½ pound (2 sticks) unsalted butter, softened
2 cups sugar
2 ½ cups all-purpose flour, sifted
½ cup sweetened condensed milk
8 egg whites

Preheat oven to 350° with the rack adjusted to the middle position. Spray two 9" cake
pans and line the bottoms with parchment paper.

In a standing mixer fitted with the paddle attachment, beat together the butter and sugar
until very fluffy on medium speed, about 4 minutes. Beat in the condensed milk and ½
cup of flour.

In a separate bowl, beat the egg whites to stiff but not dry peaks. Alternating with the
flour, in 3 additions, fold the beaten egg whites and flour into the butter and sugar mixture. Divide batter into the two cake pans.

Bake 25–30 minutes, switching the pans front to back after about 15 minutes. When the
cakes begin to pull away from the sides of the pan and a tester comes out clean, remove
pans from the oven and let cool in the pans for 10 minutes. Reverse the cakes onto
racks, remove the parchment paper and cool completely.

Pecan Cake.

1 cup butter	2½ cups flour
2 .. sugar	½ .. sweet milk
Whites 8 eggs	2 teaspoons baking powder

Beat together butter and sugar, add
a little of the beaten egg, then put in
a cup of flour, then some milk, then
again flour and milk. Put all
the milk in with the second cup
of flour, then add the rest of the
eggs.   Icing to fill and put over
top. Whites of six eggs beaten stiff
with powdered sugar, one small
can grated pineapple, and 2 cups
pecans chopped fine. The nuts should
soak while in the pine-apple before
mixing them into the egg and
sugar. Put whole pecan kernels
over the top of the cake while the
icing is still soft.

PECAN CAKE (continued)

For the filling and frosting:

1 8-ounce can finely chopped or grated pineapple
2 cups pecans, finely chopped, plus ½ cup pecan halves for garnish
6 egg whites
¼ teaspoon cream of tartar
¾ cup superfine sugar

Combine the pineapple and the finely chopped pecans and let macerate 15 minutes.

Whisk the egg whites in a large bowl or the bowl of a standing mixer fitted with the whisk attachment on medium speed until they begin to foam. Add the cream of tartar and continue to beat until soft peaks form. Slowly add the sugar, one tablespoon at a time, and continue beating on high speed until the mixture is thick, stiff, and glossy. Fold in the pineapple-nut mixture.

Place one cake layer on a serving plate and top with a layer of meringue. Top with the second layer, and ice the cake with the remaining meringue. Decorate with the pecan halves.

Serves 8–10

APPETIZERS

WARM ROSEMARY CASHEWS

1 pound roasted unsalted cashews
2 tablespoons minced fresh rosemary leaves
½ teaspoon cayenne pepper
2 teaspoons light brown sugar
2 teaspoons kosher salt
1 tablespoon unsalted butter, melted

Preheat oven to 350°.

Spread cashews on a flat pan. Toast in the oven until warm, approximately 5 minutes.

In a large bowl, combine the rosemary, cayenne pepper, sugar, salt, and butter. Add the warm cashews and toss with the spiced butter mixture.

Serve warm as an appetizer with drinks.

Yield: 2 cups

CHEESE PUFFS

¼ cup milk
1 egg
12 slices thin white bread, with crusts removed
¼ pound butter, melted
1 cup Parmesan cheese, grated

Preheat oven to 400°.

Beat egg and milk together. Dip one slice trimmed bread into egg mixture. Place it on one slice of bread that has not been dipped and top with another slice that has not been dipped, making a three-layer stack. Cut each three-layer stack into quarters.

Dip each quarter into melted butter and roll in grated cheese. Place on oiled cookie sheet. Repeat above with remaining nine slices of bread. Bake for 10 minutes, until brown.

Yield: 16 puffs

Note: Can be made early in day.

ARTICHOKE CROSTINI

1 16-ounce can artichoke hearts, drained
6 tablespoons mayonnaise
2 garlic cloves peeled, plus 2 more, peeled and cut in half, for rubbing on toast
2 tablespoons lemon juice
2 tablespoons Italian parsley, chopped
4 tablespoons grated Parmesan cheese
3 tablespoons chopped prosciutto
1 teaspoon salt
½ teaspoon black pepper
1 baguette

Preheat oven to 350°.

Blend all the ingredients, except the baguette and 2 garlic cloves, into a coarse paste in a food processor. Refrigerate until 30 minutes before ready to use. Cut baguette into diagonal slices ¾" to 1" thick. Place slices on a baking pan and toast lightly on both sides. Rub one side of the toasted slices with the remaining garlic cloves cut in half.

Spread toast thickly with room temperature artichoke mixture before serving.

Yield: 16 pieces

HERBED GARLIC PITA TOASTS

1½ sticks (¾ cup) butter, melted
1 tablespoon snipped fresh dill or 1 teaspoon dried
1 tablespoon minced fresh parsley leaves
1 large garlic clove, minced
Juice of ½ lemon
6 large pita rounds, cut in half and then separated horizontally

Preheat oven to 450°.

Combine the melted butter with the dill, parsley, garlic, and lemon juice. Brush mixture onto inside of each pita piece. Arrange buttered side up in one layer on a baking sheet. Bake for 5 minutes or until lightly browned and crisp. Cut into quarters and serve immediately.

Yield: 24 toasts

BAKED MUSHROOMS WITH CRAB

12 large mushrooms
Lemon juice
2 tablespoons butter
4 tablespoons grated Swiss cheese
¼ pound crab meat or substitute
¼ cup bread crumbs, plus additional for topping
1 tablespoon minced parsley
1 tablespoon minced onion
4 tablespoons dry sherry
Salt and pepper

Preheat oven to 350°.

Wash mushrooms. Remove stems leaving caps intact. Sprinkle a few drops of lemon juice on each cap and set aside. Mince stems very fine. Sauté in butter. Cool. Add cheese, crab, crumbs, parsley, onion and enough sherry to moisten mixture. Add salt and pepper to taste.

Pile stuffing into mushroom caps. Sprinkle with additional bread crumbs. Dot with butter and bake for 25 minutes.

Yield: 1 dozen mushrooms

"My grandparents, Cecil and Louise Gamble, moved out to Pasadena in the late 1940s. My parents, Joe and Lib Messler, and my aunt and uncle, Harriet and Jim Gamble, moved to Pasadena in 1947. I remember going to my grandparents' house at 4 Westmoreland Place throughout my childhood until my grandmother died in 1963 when I was 15. We all gathered together there for Sunday dinners at noon and on all major holidays."
—MARGARET GAMBLE MESSLER WINSLOW

SHRIMP RÉMOULADE

¼ cup Dijon mustard
½ cup olive oil
¼ cup white wine vinegar
½ teaspoon salt
¼ teaspoon pepper
2 teaspoons superfine sugar
1 tablespoon finely chopped dill
¼ cup finely chopped shallot
¼ cup chopped fresh parsley, plus additional for garnish
2½ pounds of cooked, shelled medium shrimp

Using a food processor or blender, mix all the ingredients except shrimp. Adjust seasonings to taste. Pour mixture over shrimp. Mix until blended. Chill 2–3 hours. Toss gently from time to time to make sure shrimp is well marinated. Place in a chilled bowl lined with dill or other greens.

Sprinkle with parsley and serve with cocktail picks.

Yield: 4 dozen shrimp

SPINACH AND BACON DEVILED EGGS

12 hard cooked eggs, peeled
½ cup frozen chopped spinach, thawed, drained and squeezed dry
¼ cup mayonnaise
¼ cup real bacon, cooked crisp and crumbled, about 5 strips
2½ tablespoons cider vinegar
2 tablespoons butter, softened
1 tablespoon sugar
2 teaspoons black pepper
¼ teaspoon salt

Cut eggs in half and place yolks in a bowl. Set aside halved egg whites. Mash yolks with remaining ingredients and mix well. Fill whites with mixture, piled high.

Yield: 2 dozen pieces

SPINACH-STUFFED MUSHROOMS

1 box frozen spinach soufflé, defrosted
¼ cup shredded cheddar cheese
¼ cup dried bread crumbs
¼ teaspoon dried thyme
½ teaspoon salt
16 large white or brown mushrooms, wiped and stems removed

Mix defrosted spinach soufflé with shredded cheese, bread crumbs, thyme, and salt. Microwave mixture on high for 2–2½ minutes.

Spoon microwaved mixture into prepared mushrooms. Arrange filled mushrooms on a paper towel in a Pyrex baking dish, with smaller mushrooms surrounded by larger mushrooms. Microwave on high for 3 minutes or until heated thoroughly. Serve hot.

Yield: 16 pieces

SPINACH BALLS

2 10-ounce packages frozen chopped spinach
2 cups Pepperidge Farm seasoned stuffing mix
¼ cup Parmesan cheese
1 onion, grated
¾ cup butter or margarine, melted
4 eggs, beaten
¼ teaspoon thyme
¼ teaspoon pepper
1 clove garlic, minced

Preheat oven to 350°.

Cook and drain the spinach. Squeeze out as much water as possible. Combine with the balance of the ingredients and refrigerate 2–3 hours. Form into small balls and bake on a cookie sheet for 20 minutes.

These may be frozen and reheated at 300° for about 30 minutes.

Yield: 6 dozen balls

STEAK TARTARE

½ pound top sirloin, finely ground
1 clove garlic, pressed
¼ cup capers, finely chopped
2 tablespoons parsley, finely chopped
1 egg yolk, optional
1 scallion, finely chopped
Dash Tabasco sauce
Salt and pepper to taste
Lemon juice to taste
1 teaspoon Dijon mustard
1 loaf cocktail pumpernickel bread
Unsalted butter

Mix first ten ingredients together until blended. Serve on lightly buttered pumpernickel bread slices.

Yield: ¾ cup

"When I was 10, 11 and 12 years old, my grandmother Louise, or "Bonnie" as she was known to the family, and I were especially close because of my age and because I lived so close by. The other cousins were either living in Ohio or New York; and since we all summered together in northern Michigan, the others rarely came to visit in Pasadena. My brother, Dyke, and I knew the "girls" who worked for my grandparents, especially Tony and Mildred, the upstairs maids, and Helen, one of the cooks."

—MARGARET GAMBLE MESSLER WINSLOW

VERSATILE SALMON SPREAD

1 6-ounce can salmon, boned and skinned
¼ cup labne (see note)
¼ cup mayonnaise
½ teaspoon dried dill, or ¼ teaspoon fresh dill, finely chopped
Dash of white pepper
1 tablespoon well-drained capers

In a small bowl, break up well-drained salmon with a fork. Add labne, mayonnaise, dill, and pepper. Mix well. Add capers, and mix until capers are well distributed. May be served immediately, but best after several hours or overnight in refrigerator, covered, to allow dill to release its flavor.

Serve as an appetizer with crackers or at breakfast on toasted English muffins. To serve as a light lunch, add 1 cup diced, peeled cucumber, apple or celery.

Yield: 1 cup

Note: Labne or lebni is a Lebanese yogurt-based cheese, available at Armenian or Middle Eastern markets. Its texture and flavor are between that of sour cream and traditional cream cheese. One-third cup of plain, non-sweetened yogurt may be substituted.

TUNA CONFIT

1 pound fresh tuna, cut into ⅓" slices
1 cup extra virgin olive oil
2 cloves garlic, peeled and smashed
3 sprigs fresh thyme
4 2" strips lemon peel
4 teaspoons capers, drained, plus additional for garnish
½ tablespoon minced shallots
2 tablespoons Dijon mustard
1 tablespoon sherry vinegar
½ tablespoon chicken stock
3½ tablespoons grape seed oil
Salt and pepper
Toasted country bread for serving

Place tuna in a bowl and add olive oil, garlic, thyme, and lemon peel. Cover and marinate 6 hours or overnight, refrigerated or at room temperature.

Transfer contents of the bowl to a saucepan, bring to a simmer, lower heat, and cook 5 minutes. Shut off heat. Tuna will still be pink in the middle. Let cool about 30 minutes.

Remove tuna, drain well, transfer to a bowl and mash coarsely with a fork. Fold capers, shallots, mustard, and sherry vinegar into tuna. Whisk 2 tablespoons of the olive oil with the chicken stock and grape seed oil. Fold into the tuna mixture. Season with salt and pepper. Mixture will be fairly loose.

Serve at once, placing mounds of tuna on each of 4 salad plates. Sprinkle with more capers and serve with toast as a first course; or refrigerate tuna until 30 minutes before serving, then divide onto plates and serve.

Yield: 8 servings as appetizer or 4 servings as salad

SMOKED SALMON DEVILED EGGS

¼ pound smoked salmon, coarsely chopped
2 tablespoons light cream cheese
2 tablespoons mayonnaise
2 teaspoons lemon juice
Freshly ground white or black pepper
4 large eggs, hard-cooked, peeled and halved lengthwise

Place the salmon, cream cheese, mayonnaise and lemon juice in the bowl of a food processor. Pulse 3–4 times until blended. Add 3 or 4 grinds of pepper and pulse once to combine.

Remove and discard, or save, cooked egg yolks for another purpose. Place egg halves, cut side up, on a plate. With a spoon, scoop up enough salmon filling to make balls the size of an egg yolk. Roll the balls lightly between your fingers to shape. Set them in the cooked egg whites. Serve chilled. May be garnished with watercress or parsley sprigs.

Yield: 8 pieces

PETITE REUBENS

½ pint sauerkraut
I loaf cocktail rye bread
Mustard
½ pound cold lean corned beef, thinly sliced
½ pound Swiss cheese, sliced paper thin

Preheat oven to 400°.

Squeeze sauerkraut until excess liquid has been removed. Set aside.

Spread each slice of bread generously with mustard.

Top with folded slice of corned beef that covers bread but does not extend over edges.

Spread about ½ teaspoon sauerkraut over meat, and top with folded piece of Swiss cheese, slightly larger than bread.

Bake for about 4 minutes or until cheese is melted.

Note: May be frozen after cooking and reheated before serving. Keeps about 3 months.

Yield: 3 dozen

VODKA TOMATOES OR "BLOODY MARY ON A STICK"

I basket of firm, ripe cherry tomatoes
½ cup ice-cold premium vodka
¼ cup kosher salt
Cocktail toothpicks

Bring about 3 cups of water to a boil. Plunge the tomatoes into the boiling water for 20 seconds. Remove from water and plunge into ice water for 10 seconds. Drain. Peel the tomatoes and place in a bowl. Cover with plastic film and refrigerate.

When ready to serve, place the tomatoes on a rimmed platter. Pour the ice-cold vodka over the tomatoes to almost cover. Serve tomatoes with toothpicks and salt in a small bowl.

Spear a tomato with a toothpick and dip the tomato in the salt.

Yield: 20–25 tomatoes

SALADS

AVOCADO AND MUSHROOM SALAD

2 avocados
½ pound small mushroom caps

Peel and slice avocados. Wipe mushrooms clean. Remove stems and reserve for another use. Combine avocado slices and mushroom caps. Prepare the following dressing:

½ cup oil
3 tablespoons tarragon vinegar
2 tablespoons lemon juice
2 tablespoons water
1 tablespoon parsley, chopped
1 clove garlic, minced
¾ teaspoon salt
Freshly ground pepper

Combine all of the above and pour over the avocado slices and mushroom caps. Chill several hours, stirring the vegetables several times. Arrange attractively on lettuce leaves.

Yield: 8 servings

ROASTED CHICKEN AND CRANBERRY SALAD

½ cup dried cranberries, chopped
4 tablespoons olive oil
1½ tablespoons fresh lime juice
1 pound cooked, smoked chicken breast, cut in ½" dice (3 cups)
⅓ cup sliced almonds, toasted
4 ribs celery, diced
Salt and pepper to taste
2 cups mixed greens

Mix all ingredients except greens and serve on a bed of mixed greens.

Yield: 4 servings

SHREDDED CARROT AND NAPA CABBAGE SALAD

1 pound carrots, shredded
¾ pound Napa cabbage, shredded

Dressing:
3 tablespoons rice vinegar
⅓ cup peanut oil
2 tablespoons minced parsley
2 tablespoons sesame oil
Salt to taste

Combine carrots and cabbage. Pour dressing over and toss. Chill 30 minutes.

Yield: 8 servings

CHINESE RICE CURRY SALAD

1 cup rice
1 cup minced onion
1 jar marinated artichokes (6 ounces), undrained and chopped
2 tablespoons vinegar
2 teaspoons salt
1½ teaspoons curry powder
2 cups celery, chopped
1 cup chicken, chopped
⅓ cup sour cream
⅓ cup mayonnaise
1 cup petite frozen peas, defrosted

Cook rice according to package directions. Mix with onion, artichokes, vinegar, salt, and curry powder. Chill for 3 hours or overnight. Add remaining ingredients to rice mixture and mix well. Chill thoroughly for one hour.

Yield: 15 4-ounce servings

OVERNIGHT CABBAGE AND PEA SALAD

1 small cabbage, shredded
1 green onion, thinly sliced
2 stalks celery, thinly sliced
2 tablespoons minced parsley
1 10-ounce package frozen peas, unthawed
1 teaspoon sugar

Layer the vegetables in a bowl and sprinkle with sugar. Prepare with the following dressing:

¾ cup mayonnaise
½ cup sour cream
1 tablespoon Dijon mustard
1 tablespoon red wine vinegar
1 teaspoon salt
1 teaspoon curry powder, or to taste

Combine the ingredients well. Spread dressing on top of the vegetables to the edges of the bowl.

Cover and refrigerate the salad overnight. Mix well about 5 minutes before serving.

Yield: 6–8 servings

FROZEN CRANBERRY AND PINEAPPLE SALAD

1 16-ounce can whole cranberry sauce
1 8¼-ounce can crushed pineapple in syrup
1 cup sour cream
¼ cup powdered sugar

Combine cranberry sauce and pineapple. Stir the sour cream and sugar together and combine with cranberry mixture. Pour into a foil-lined 8" x 8" pan and freeze until firm. Remove from freezer. Cut into 9–12 portions. Serve frozen on salad plates or platter.

Yield: 9–12 servings

WINTER FRUIT SALAD

1 red apple, peeled, cored, and thinly sliced
2 ripe pears, peeled, cored, and quartered
1 cup seedless grapes
1 cup orange or tangerine sections, plus one orange, thinly sliced for garnish
½ cup sliced dates, plus 8 whole pitted dates reserved for garnish
½ cup thinly sliced celery
⅓ cup currant or guava jelly
1 tablespoon fresh lemon juice
Crisp bibb lettuce

In a large bowl, combine the first 6 salad ingredients. Beat the jelly and lemon juice until well blended. Toss with fruit and celery until well coated. Arrange lettuce on plates, mound salad in center and garnish with thin slices of orange and whole dates. Serve well chilled.

Yield: 8 servings

SALAD OLÉ

1 pound ground beef
Dash of hot sauce to taste
1 15-ounce can kidney beans, drained
1 onion, chopped
4 tomatoes, cut in pieces
1 head lettuce, torn
4 ounces grated cheddar cheese
8 ounces thousand island or California onion dressing
1 avocado, sliced or cubed
1 bag of tortilla chips, crushed

Brown ground beef with hot sauce and add kidney beans. Simmer 10 minutes. Cool to room temperature and mix with next 5 ingredients. Just before serving add tortilla chips and sprinkle with cheese.

Yield: 8–10 servings

Note: Use unsalted tortilla chips if desired.

CANTONESE CHICKEN SALAD

5 cups diced, cooked chicken
I cup chopped celery
½ cup chopped green onions
I 8-ounce can sliced water chestnuts
2 cups drained pineapple chunks, cut in half
I 3-ounce can Chinese noodles
½ cup slivered almonds

Dressing:
4 tablespoons chopped chutney
I cup mayonnaise
I cup sour cream
I teaspoon curry powder

In a large bowl mix chicken, celery, sliced onions and water chestnuts with dressing and chill at least one hour before serving. Add pineapple and noodles at the last minute. Toss and top with almonds. Garnish with slices of cantaloupe, clusters of green grapes and strawberries, if desired.

Yield: 8 servings

BLACK-EYED PEA AND RICE SALAD

2 10-ounce packages frozen black-eyed peas
1½ cups long-grain rice, raw
¼ cup cider vinegar
I teaspoon ground cumin
I teaspoon minced garlic
I teaspoon salt
1½ teaspoons freshly ground pepper
⅓ cup olive oil
2 cups chopped celery
I 10-ounce package frozen whole kernel corn, thawed
½ cup finely chopped red onion
½ cup chopped fresh cilantro
2 tablespoons minced, seeded jalapeño peppers

Cook black-eyed peas 20 minutes in a large pot of boiling salted water. Then drain.

Cook rice according to package directions; rinse in sieve under warm water and drain.

Meanwhile, whisk vinegar, cumin, garlic, salt and pepper together in large bowl. Gradually whisk in oil. Add warm peas and rice and toss to coat. Add remaining ingredients and toss well. Serve at room temperature or chilled.

Yield: 6 servings

Note: If jalapeños are too hot, use a milder type such as New Mexico chile.

MALAYSIAN MIXED FRUIT AND VEGETABLE SALAD

1 cup peeled, unripened green mango flesh, cut into ¾" cubes
1 cup peeled jicama, cut into ¾" cubes
1 fresh pineapple, cut into ½" cubes
1 7-ounce peeled, seeded cucumber, cut into ¾" cubes
1¼ cups washed and dried bean sprouts
1½ cups chopped peanuts
1½ tablespoons toasted sesame seeds

Dressing:
1 cup dark soy sauce
6 tablespoons dark molasses
3 tablespoons dark brown sugar
2 tablespoons lime juice
¼ teaspoon cayenne pepper (several drops of Tabasco sauce may be substituted)

Combine first 4 ingredients in large bowl.

Scatter bean sprouts over cubed fruit. Cover with plastic wrap and refrigerate until ready to serve.

Mix soy sauce, molasses, and brown sugar in small saucepan. Heat until sugar is dissolved. Set aside to cool. When cool, mix 6–7 tablespoons of sauce with 1½–2 tablespoons lime juice and ⅛–¼ teaspoon cayenne pepper. Set aside until ready to serve. When ready to serve, pour dressing over fruit and vegetables and toss gently. Scatter peanuts and sesame seeds over salad and serve.

Yields: 4–6 servings

GREEN BEAN AND CHEESE SALAD

14 ounces green beans, cut into 1" pieces
1 cup grated Gruyere cheese
2 ounces shallots, minced (4 large shallots)
2 tablespoons olive oil
2 tablespoons red wine vinegar
1 tablespoon grainy Dijon mustard
¼ teaspoon salt
⅛ teaspoon black pepper

Blanch the green beans in boiling salted water for 5 minutes. Drain and run under cold water to stop the cooking. Drain well and combine with the cheese in a large mixing bowl.

Whisk together all remaining ingredients for dressing. Combine with the green beans and cheese. Mix well.

Yield: 6 servings

WARM PASTA SALAD WITH VEGETABLES

9 ounces fresh fettucine, cut in 2" pieces
⅔ cup chopped fresh basil
2 cups chopped broccoli florets
3 chopped Italian tomatoes
1 cubed avocado
1 bunch chopped green onions
2 cups chopped, mixed peppers, green, red and yellow
1 cup sliced mushrooms

Dressing:
1 teaspoon Dijon mustard
½ cup wine vinegar
3 tablespoon olive oil
Salt and pepper to taste

Bring pot of water to boil. Cook and drain pasta.

Put vegetables in large bowl. Mix dressing ingredients together. Add hot pasta and dressing to vegetables and toss.

Yield: 4-6 main dish servings

Note: Fresh fettucine is available in refrigerated cases in better markets. Use other vegetables and chopped chicken, turkey and cheese for variety.

OVERNIGHT LAYERED SALAD

Salad:
1 large head lettuce, chopped
1 romaine lettuce, chopped
1 bunch green onions, chopped
1 green pepper, chopped
1 bunch celery, chopped
2 cans water chestnuts, sliced and drained
2 cups cooked chopped ham
1 large package frozen peas, thawed
Parmesan cheese

Dressing:
1 cup mayonnaise
1 cup sour cream
1 teaspoon each sugar, garlic salt, seasoned salt and lemon juice

In a large salad bowl layer the salad ingredients in the order listed and repeat. Combine dressing ingredients and spread over the salad, sealing it to the edges of the bowl. Sprinkle with cheese, cover with plastic wrap, and refrigerate overnight.

Mix well before serving.

Yield: 10–12 servings

WHITE BEAN SALAD

1 pound navy beans or any small white beans
4 green onions, including tops, chopped
10 ripe olives, minced
10 stuffed green olives, sliced
½ cup olive oil
¼ cup salad oil
¼ cup white wine vinegar
½ teaspoon dried basil or 1½ tablespoons fresh basil
2 cloves garlic, minced
Salt and pepper
1 tomato, optional
1 egg, hard boiled, optional

Wash beans and soak in cold water for 2 hours. Bring beans and water to a boil and simmer the beans, partly covered, until they are tender but not mushy. Drain and toss with the onions and olives. Mix together the oils, vinegar, garlic and seasonings. Add to bean mixture and mix gently. Garnish with quartered eggs and tomato if desired.

Yield: 8 servings

Note: Two cans of white beans, drained and rinsed, may be substituted for the navy beans.

TABBOULEH SALAD

1 cup chopped flat leaf parsley, approximately 1 bunch, chopped medium to fine
¾ cup mint, chopped medium to fine
½ cup finely sliced green tomatoes
6–8 Roma tomatoes, cut into medium to small dice
¾ cup cracked bulgur wheat, grade #2
Juice of 1–2 lemons
½ cup extra virgin olive oil
1 tablespoon ground cinnamon
Kosher salt, to taste
Romaine lettuce leaves, optional

Soak cracked bulgur wheat in ¾ cup warm water until all moisture is absorbed into the wheat. Wheat should be semi-soft. Combine all ingredients together in a mixing bowl and mix gently. Let stand until wheat is soft, approximately 10 minutes. Serve on lettuce leaves if desired.

Yield: 6–8 servings

Note: The amounts do not have to be exact.

CRUNCHY PEA SALAD

1 16-ounce package frozen green peas
2 eggs, hard boiled and chopped
1 8-ounce can sliced water chestnuts, drained or 1 cup julienned jicama
2 tablespoons chopped pimiento
⅓ cup sliced scallions
½ cup sliced celery
½ cup mayonnaise
1 tablespoon Dijon mustard
½ teaspoon garlic salt
¼ teaspoon pepper
Lettuce leaves

Blanch the peas. Drain and refresh with cold water and drain well again. Combine the eggs and vegetables. Stir in the mayonnaise, mustard, and other seasonings. Mix together gently.

Cover and chill overnight. Serve on lettuce leaves.

Yield: 6 servings

ROQUEFORT APRICOT SALAD

12 apricot halves, canned or fresh
3 tablespoons lemon juice
½ cup Roquefort cheese, room temperature
1 3-ounce package cream cheese, softened
3 tablespoons butter, softened
1 tablespoon sherry
Chopped pistachio nuts

Drain the fruit and turn cut side up. Sprinkle with lemon juice. Whip the cheeses and butter until smooth. Add the sherry and pipe the mixture in rosettes into the apricot halves. Sprinkle with nuts.

Yield: 4 servings

WATERCRESS SALAD

¼ cup pecans
1 bunch watercress, washed and dried
2–6 green onions, thinly sliced
1 8-ounce can of mandarin oranges, chilled and drained

Dressing:
3 tablespoons olive oil
3 tablespoons lemon juice
1½ teaspoons Dijon mustard
Salt and pepper

Preheat oven to 350°. Roast pecans in shallow pan in single layer until fragrant and slightly browned, about 5–7 minutes. Cool.

Tear watercress into bite-sized pieces. Mix dressing ingredients with whisk.

Put watercress in bowl. Add mandarin oranges and onions. Break pecans and add to salad bowl. Toss with dressing.

Yield: 4 servings

SOUPS

GOOD SOUP

Canola oil
1 pound lean ground beef
1 onion, coarsely chopped
1 cup sliced celery
1 medium potato, cubed
1 15-ounce can chopped tomatoes
2 teaspoons beef bouillon powder dissolved in 2 cups water
½ teaspoon kosher salt
1 teaspoon freshly ground black pepper
1 teaspoon chili powder
1 16-ounce can red kidney beans, drained
2 cups thinly shredded cabbage

Brown beef in an oiled Dutch oven, stirring beef until brown and crumbly. Add onion and celery. Sauté for 5 minutes. Stir in potatoes, tomatoes, water with bouillon, salt, chili powder, and pepper. Cover and simmer until potatoes are tender. Bring to a boil. Add beans and cabbage. Cover and cook until cabbage is tender, about 3 minutes. This makes for a very hearty soup, about the consistency of chili.

If you prefer a thinner soup, add one 14-ounce can of vegetable broth or low-sodium chicken stock, and cook 5–8 minutes.

Yield: 6 servings

ARTICHOKE SOUP

Soup:
2 tablespoons olive oil
1–2 onions, chopped
2 tablespoons flour
1–2 cloves garlic, chopped
6 cups chicken broth
2–3 boxes frozen artichoke hearts, defrosted
1 teaspoon dried tarragon
Salt and white pepper
½ cup sour cream

Heat 2 tablespoons of oil in a sauté pan. Add onions and flour to the oil. Stir until flour is cooked and onions have softened, then add garlic and sauté, stirring, for 1 minute over medium heat. Add broth and bring to boil. Add artichokes and simmer for about 30 minutes. Purée soup and add tarragon, salt and pepper to taste. Serve in bowls or mugs. Top with a spoonful of sour cream and a spoonful of gremolata.

Gremolata:
½ cup chopped parsley
Finely grated zest of 2 lemons
3 cloves of garlic, minced
Salt and pepper
1 tablespoon olive oil

Mix ingredients together until well blended.

Yield: 6 servings

ASPARAGUS SOUP

1¼ cups leeks (white and pale green part only), about 6–8 medium leeks
2 tablespoons unsalted butter
½ cup chopped shallots
¾ teaspoon salt
¼ teaspoon pepper
1 quart chicken broth
1 cup water
2½ pounds asparagus, trimmed and cut into 1" pieces (reserve tips for garnish)
½ cup heavy cream
Parmesan cheese for garnish

Cut leeks in half lengthwise, rinse under running water, and chop leeks coarsely. Melt butter in a 4– to 6– quart pot over moderate heat. Add leeks and shallots, ½ teaspoon salt, and pepper and cook, stirring, until leek is softened. Add water and broth. Bring to boil. Add asparagus to pot and cook, covered, for approximately 6–8 minutes, until asparagus is tender. Purée soup. Add cream and check for seasoning. Heat over moderately low heat until hot. Garnish with asparagus tips. Finely grate fresh Parmesan and float on top of soup in the bowl.

Yield: 6 servings

CREAM OF AVOCADO SOUP

2 large ripe avocados
2 cups cold chicken stock
1 cup heavy cream
1 teaspoon grated onion
Salt and freshly ground pepper
Pinch of curry powder

Peel and seed the avocados. Cube enough avocado to make ¼ cup and set aside for a garnish. Blend the remaining avocados, stock, cream, and onion until smooth. Season to taste with salt and pepper and a bit of curry. Serve cold, garnished with the reserved avocado cubes.

Yield: 4 servings

BUTTERNUT SQUASH BISQUE

4 tablespoons butter
1 leek, white part only, sliced
1 onion, chopped
1 tablespoon flour
1 medium butternut squash, peeled and diced
2 cups chicken broth
2–3 tablespoons vermouth or dry sherry
Pinch of herbs of choice
Dash of freshly grated nutmeg
1 cup cream
½ cup chopped parsley

Melt butter in a large saucepan and slowly sauté leek and onion until translucent. Stir in flour and cook 1 minute. Add squash and broth to cover. Simmer, partially covered, until squash is soft, about 20 minutes. Cool slightly and add the vermouth or sherry. Purée; return to pan and season with herbs and nutmeg. Stir in cream slowly until the desired consistency. Heat to serving temperature. Do not boil. Sprinkle with parsley before serving.

Yield: 5–6 servings

BUTTERNUT SQUASH AND CORN SOUP

2 pounds butternut squash
2 tablespoons olive oil, plus extra for browning garnish
1 large onion, cut in ½" cubes
1 medium leek, sliced and washed twice
2 cups frozen corn kernels or 4 ears of fresh corn scraped off cob
1 teaspoon salt
5 cups chicken broth
2 branches fresh rosemary (or 1 teaspoon dried)

Peel squash and cut into ½" cubes. Heat olive oil in stockpot and sauté onion and leek over medium heat, about 5 minutes. Add squash and corn (reserving 2 tablespoons of corn for garnish) and sauté an additional 10 minutes. Add broth, rosemary and salt and cook uncovered for an additional 30 minutes, until squash is soft. Drain and reserve half of the stock. Remove rosemary branches. In a processor or blender, purée the vegetables with the remaining stock. Add more of the reserved stock until desired consistency is reached.

Garnish: Brown the reserved 2 tablespoons of corn kernels in an oil-coated skillet to use as garnish on top of each serving.

Yield: 6 servings

"Sometimes after lunch, my grandfather took my brother and me upstairs to the third floor to see what was going on in the nesting cages. Another treat was to go with him to feed the birds outside in the three very large cages, each six feet square and maybe seven to eight feet tall. Occasionally he let us go into the cages. I think my grandfather was happiest when attending to his beloved birds, and I was honored that he allowed me to come with him inside the cages. Other cages were below the fish pond and lawn, not quite visible from the house, although you could easily hear the chirping from the house."

—MARGARET GAMBLE MESSLER WINSLOW

FRUIT GAZPACHO

2 cups tomato purée
3 cups orange juice
2 teaspoons sugar
Grated zest of 1 orange
Grated zest of 1 lime
2 cups cantaloupe, diced
2 cups honeydew, diced
1 mango, peeled and diced
1 apple, peeled and diced
1 cup fresh blueberries
1 cup halved red or green grapes
Strawberries or kiwi slices

Combine purée, juice, sugar, zests, melons, and mango. Process half of this mixture in a blender or food processor until smooth. Stir the purée into the unpuréed mixture and stir to combine. Add all of the fruits except the strawberries and kiwis. Chill for several hours.

Serve in chilled bowls garnished with the strawberries and kiwi slices.

Yield: 8 servings

SUMMER GRAPE-CUCUMBER SOUP

5 cucumbers, peeled, seeded, halved
½ pound green seedless grapes
2 ice cubes
½ red onion, minced
2 small serrano chiles, peeled and minced (optional)
3 tablespoons chopped cilantro
2 teaspoons lime juice
1 tablespoon champagne vinegar
1 tablespoon sugar
Salt and pepper

Purée 2 cucumbers with the grapes, reserving 12 grape halves for garnish, and ice cubes in a food processor, and pour into a bowl. Dice remaining cucumbers. Add remaining cucumbers, onion, chilies and cilantro to the purée in the bowl. Add lime juice, vinegar, salt and pepper and sugar. Cover and chill thoroughly, at least 3 hours.

Garnish with reserved grapes.

Yield: 4-6 servings

DELICIOUS MUSHROOM BISQUE

12 cups (2 pounds) assorted fresh mushrooms (portabella, porcini, or chanterelles), cleaned and chopped
2 tablespoons unsalted butter
4 quarts vegetable stock
1 bay leaf
2 large garlic cloves, minced
1 cup dry sherry
8 cups heavy cream or half-and-half (not as rich)
Salt and fresh ground white pepper
Chopped parsley for garnish

In Dutch oven, sauté mushrooms in butter over medium heat for 5 minutes. Remove from heat. Set aside to cool for 15 minutes, and transfer mushrooms to food processor and process until finely chopped. Set aside.

In a large stockpot, combine the vegetable stock, bay leaf, and garlic. Bring to a boil over medium heat until the mixture is reduced by half, about 45 minutes. Add sherry and heavy cream or half-and-half. Remove bay leaf and stir constantly over medium heat until the mixture is reduced by half, about 30 minutes. Do not let boil.

Add mushroom purée and warm thoroughly over low heat. Season with salt and pepper to taste.

Serve immediately in soup tureen or divide among individual soup plates. Garnish with parsley.

Yield: 10–12 servings

PEANUT BUTTER SOUP

1 teaspoon minced onion
1 tablespoon butter
3 tablespoons smooth peanut butter
2 tablespoons flour
3 cups scalded milk
Salt and pepper
¾ cup coarsely chopped salted peanuts

In a heavy saucepan, cook onion in butter and peanut butter for 5 minutes. Add flour and stir until smooth. Slowly add scalded milk. Cook 20 minutes in a double boiler. Season to taste with salt and pepper. Garnish each serving with a sprinkle of chopped salted peanuts.

Yield: 6 servings

ASIAN TURKEY NOODLE SOUP WITH GINGER

3½ ounces medium-wide rice noodles (linguine width), broken into 6" lengths
Boiling water
6 cups turkey broth or chicken broth, homemade or canned
½ cup thinly sliced shallots
1½" peeled fresh ginger, sliced into 10 rounds
2 tablespoons fish sauce (nam pla or nuoc nam) or soy sauce
2 cups diced or shredded cooked turkey (about 10–12 ounces)

Garnishes:
Fresh bean sprouts
Fresh mint leaves
Fresh cilantro
Thickly sliced serrano chiles
Lime wedges

Place noodles in large bowl. Add enough boiling water to cover. Let stand until noodles are soft, about 5 minutes. Drain.

Combine broth, shallots, ginger, and fish sauce in a large pot. Bring to a boil. Reduce heat to low, cover partially, and simmer 10 minutes. Discard ginger slices. Return broth to boil. Stir in noodles and turkey and simmer until turkey is heated through, about 3 minutes.

Ladle soup into bowls. Serve, allowing diners to choose garnishes.

Yield: 4–6 servings

GAMBLE HOUSE PUMPKIN SOUP

¼ cup finely chopped onion
2 tablespoons butter or oil
¼ teaspoon curry powder, or to taste
1 14-ounce can chicken broth
1 15-ounce can pumpkin purée
½ teaspoon salt
⅛ teaspoon pepper
Whipped cream or plain yogurt for garnish
Roasted pumpkin seeds or pine nuts for garnish

In a heavy 2-quart saucepan, sauté onions in butter or oil until tender. Add curry powder and stir until fragrant. Add chicken broth and bring to boil. Lower heat to medium-high. Add pumpkin, ½ teaspoon salt and ⅛ teaspoon pepper. Stir well and bring almost to a boil. Lower heat and simmer about 20 minutes. Adjust seasoning.

Optional: At this point you can purée soup with an immersion blender to incorporate the onions for a smoother soup.

Serve in bowls with a dollop of unsweetened whipped cream or plain yogurt. Sprinkle roasted pumpkin seeds or pine nuts on top.

Yield: 2–4 servings

HEARTY POTATO-LEEK SOUP

2 medium russet potatoes, peeled and diced
2 cloves garlic
7 cups water
2 turnips, coarsely shredded
2 medium carrots, coarsely shredded
6 tablespoons butter
2 leeks, white part only, thinly sliced
1 cup cream
Thyme, salt and pepper
Parsley

In a large saucepan, simmer the potatoes and garlic in the water. Sauté the turnips, carrots and leeks in the butter to soften and then add to the potato pot. When all vegetables are cooked, about 10 minutes, add the cream, adjust the seasonings and heat to serving temperature. Do not boil. Garnish with parsley if desired.

Yield: 6 servings

TUSCAN BREAD SOUP

4–6 slices crusty Italian or French bread (sourdough is good for this)
4 tablespoons extra virgin olive oil, plus extra for drizzling
1 large onion, finely chopped
6 cloves garlic, minced
6 cups low-sodium chicken broth
½ cup heavy cream
1 teaspoon minced fresh rosemary
½ cup grated Parmesan cheese

Adjust oven rack to middle position and heat oven to 475°.

Place bread slices on baking sheet and brush each top with 1 tablespoon olive oil. Bake until golden brown and crusty (8–10 minutes). Set aside.

Heat remaining 3 tablespoons olive oil in a Dutch oven over medium heat until shimmering. Add onion and cook until soft and lightly browned, about 8 minutes. Add garlic and cook 30 seconds, being careful not to burn. Add broth, cream, and rosemary. Simmer 10–12 minutes. Add salt and pepper to taste.

Cut toast into 1" cubes and place in soup bowls. Ladle soup over bread. Sprinkle generously with Parmesan cheese and drizzle with olive oil.

Yield: 4–6 servings

SUPER SIMPLE FRENCH ONION SOUP

3 tablespoons butter (do not use substitutes)
2 large onions, thinly sliced
1 tablespoon flour
½ teaspoon salt
2 10½-ounce cans beef bouillon (not bouillon cubes)
4 1"-thick slices French bread
4 tablespoons grated Parmesan cheese

Melt butter in a deep saucepan. Add onions and sauté over medium high heat until they are caramelized (golden brown, soft, and clear), stirring frequently to prevent burning. This step will take 20-30 minutes.

Sprinkle flour over the onions, stir and cook 1 minute longer. Add salt and bouillon. Simmer, covered, for 20 minutes. Adjust seasonings.

Toast bread slices on one side in the broiler. Turn slices over and sprinkle cheese on each one. Toast, cheese side up, until cheese is lightly browned. Place a piece of cheese toast in each bowl and pour soup over the toast. Serve immediately.

This recipe can be doubled or tripled.

Yield: 4 servings

Note: It's a good idea to make extra cheese toasts as most people like second helpings.

ZUCCHINI SOUP

9 cups zucchini, sliced (about 3 pounds)
1 onion, chopped
1 13¾-ounce can chicken consommé or stock, plus 2 cans water
1 teaspoon salt
1 teaspoon seasoning salt
1 teaspoon dried basil
¼ teaspoon pepper
5 slices bacon
Parmesan cheese

Place all ingredients, except bacon and cheese, in a large kettle and simmer for 30 minutes. Let cool slightly. Purée in small batches in a blender. Cook the bacon until crisp. Drain and crumble. Bring soup back to serving temperature and garnish with the bacon and Parmesan cheese.

Yield: 8 servings

VICHYSSOISE

1 tablespoon butter
2 tablespoons olive oil
2 leeks, whites only
1 Maui (sweet) onion, diced
4 potatoes, peeled
1–2 quarts chicken stock
Cream or half-and-half, to taste
½ cup minced chives and parsley

Melt butter and oil together in a skillet over medium high heat. Sauté diced leeks and onions until translucent. Set aside. Boil diced potatoes in 1 quart chicken stock until tender. Let cool and purée with the cooled vegetables. The soup can be refrigerated overnight; it will be thick when cold. Dilute with remaining chicken stock and cream to desired thickness.

Garnish with minced herbs.

Yield: 8 servings

BREADS

HOT PUMPKIN BISCUITS

2 cups all-purpose flour
3 tablespoons sugar
4 teaspoons baking powder
½ teaspoon salt
½ teaspoon cinnamon
½ cup cold butter, cut up into ½" cubes
⅓ cup chopped pecans
½ cup half-and-half
⅔ cup mashed pumpkin

Preheat oven to 450°.

Sift together dry ingredients. Cut in butter to make coarse crumbs. Stir in pecans. Combine half-and-half with pumpkin. Add pumpkin mixture to dry ingredients to make a stiff dough.

Turn out dough onto a floured board and knead a few times. Roll out ½" thick. Use a 2" cutter to cut biscuits. Bake 1" apart on a lightly greased baking sheet for 20 minutes. Serve hot.

Yield: 20 biscuits

BRIOCHE

2 cups flour
¼ ounce active dry yeast
¼ cup water at 105°
3 tablespoons sugar
1 teaspoon salt
2 eggs
4 ounces butter
1 yolk, beaten

Proof yeast with water and 1 tablespoon sugar. Place flour, salt and remaining 2 tablespoons sugar in a large bowl, making a well in the center. Add yeast mixture and break eggs into center of well.

Mix eggs and yeast by hand, gradually pulling flour in from sides until all flour has been moistened. The dough should be soft and sticky.

Turn out onto floured work surface. Using both hands and a pastry scraper, knead dough thoroughly for 30 minutes. Dough should be smooth and elastic and lose all of its stickiness. (You may use a mixer with dough hook. It will take about 10–15 minutes.)

Cut butter into tablespoons and cut into dough with scraper until thoroughly blended. Place dough in a large buttered bowl until doubled in bulk, about 1 hour. Cover with plastic wrap.

Punch dough down. Knead lightly. Place back in bowl and let rise again, about 45 minutes. Chill 30 minutes and then shape. Brush top with remaining egg yolk.

Bake at 350° in well-oiled 9" x 5" loaf pan until golden and dry in center, about 45 minutes.

Yield: 1 loaf

GREEN CHILI SPOON BREAD

1 cup corn meal
½ teaspoon salt
3 teaspoons baking powder
3 beaten eggs
1 16-ounce can creamed corn
1 cup buttermilk
½ cup vegetable oil
1 4-ounce can chopped Ortega green chiles
2 cups grated sharp cheddar cheese

Preheat oven to 350°.

Mix dry ingredients. Mix remaining ingredients except the chiles and cheese. Add to the dry mixture and blend. Pour half of batter into greased 9" x 9" pan.

Sprinkle with half the cheese and chiles. Pour remaining batter over this and top with other half of cheese and chiles. Bake for 1 hour. Cut into squares.

Yield: 8 servings

Note: Alternatively, you can mix the chiles in with the batter. This method makes the distribution of the chiles more even.

ENGLISH NUT BREAD

4 cups sifted flour
4 teaspoons baking powder
1 teaspoon salt
1 cup sugar
2 cups chopped walnut meats
1 egg, well-beaten
1¾ cups milk

Preheat oven to 350°.

Mix and sift dry ingredients. Stir in nuts. Combine milk and beaten egg and add to flour mixture, stirring only until blended. Turn into greased 9" x 5" loaf pan and let stand 20–30 minutes.

Bake for 50 minutes. Test center with bamboo skewer. Remove from pan to cool and place on cooking rack. When cool, wrap in foil and store.

For best results, let stand 24 hours before slicing thinly. Serve with butter.

Yield: 1 loaf

Note: This is a Greene family favorite.

GOLDEN RAISIN, FENNEL, AND CORNMEAL BREAD

1 teaspoon active dry yeast
1 teaspoon sugar
¾ cup lukewarm milk
1 tablespoon fine sea salt
1 tablespoon extra virgin olive oil
2¼ cups lukewarm water
1 tablespoon fennel seed
6 cups bread flour (approximately)
2 cups coarse, yellow cornmeal, plus extra for pan
¾ cup golden raisins

In the bowl of a heavy-duty mixer fitted with a paddle, combine yeast, sugar and milk. Stir to blend. Let stand covered until foamy, about 5 minutes. Add salt, oil, water, and fennel seed and stir to blend.

On low speed, add about 2 cups of the flour to the mixing bowl, a little at a time, mixing well after each addition. Add cornmeal a little at a time, mixing well after each addition. Add raisins. Add remaining flour a little at a time on low speed, just until most of the flour has been absorbed and the dough begins to form a ball. Continue to mix for 5 minutes on the lowest speed. Cover the bowl with plastic wrap and refrigerate for at least 8 hours or overnight until the dough doubles in size.

Remove dough from the refrigerator, punch it down, and cover again with plastic wrap. Let rise at room temperature until doubled in size, about 2–3 hours. Punch down dough and knead about 30 seconds. Shape the dough into 2 tight balls.

Sprinkle a cookie sheet with cornmeal and place the balls of dough, seam side down, on the sheet with space between the balls. Loosely fold a clean damp cloth over the dough. Let rise at room temperature until doubled in size, about 1¼ hours. With a razor or very sharp knife, slash the top of each loaf 2–3 times.

At least 40 minutes before the dough has finished rising, preheat oven to 475°. Place bread in oven and with a plant mister, spray the center of the oven. Bread will not turn soggy; the steam helps give a good crust. Then spray 3 more times during the first 6 minutes of baking. Once the bread is lightly browned, about 10 minutes, lower the heat to 400° and rotate the loaves so they brown evenly. Bake until the crust is a deep, golden brown and sounds hollow when tapped on the bottom, about another 20–25 minutes, for a total baking time of about 30–35 minutes.

Remove loaves from oven and place on rack to cool. Bread will continue to bake as it rests. Do not cut for at least 1 hour. Bread can be stored in air-tight wrapping for 3–4 days.

Yield: 2 medium loaves

JALAPEÑO CORN BREAD

1 cup cream-style corn
1 cup corn meal
⅔ cup salad oil
1 tablespoon baking powder
2 eggs, beaten
1 cup sour cream
1 teaspoon salt
1 cup grated cheese
1 4-ounce can diced jalapeño peppers, drained

Preheat oven to 350°.

Mix all of the ingredients except the cheese and peppers. Pour half the batter into a greased 8" square pan. Sprinkle with the peppers and half the cheese. Add the remaining batter and top with the balance of the cheese.

Bake for 1 hour. This may also be baked in an iron skillet that has been heated before adding the batter.

Yield: 6 servings

HONEY WHITE BREAD

1 cup lukewarm water
2 quarter-ounce packages active dry yeast
1½ cups lukewarm milk
3 tablespoons honey
2 teaspoons sea salt
⅓ cup vegetable oil
6-7 cups all-purpose flour, plus extra for shaping dough

In a large mixer bowl, sprinkle yeast over warm water, stir, and allow it to stand 2–3 minutes to dissolve. Add milk, honey, salt, oil, and 3 cups flour. Using dough hook (or a wooden spoon to stir), blend at low speed until thoroughly mixed. Add remaining flour, ½ cup at a time. Amount of flour to be added will depend on flour. Add only enough to form a ball. Knead with dough hook for about 5 minutes or with hands until dough is shiny and elastic. Shape dough into 2 balls. Allow to rest for 10 minutes covered with a clean towel. Oil two 9" x 5" loaf pans.

On a floured surface, roll each ball of dough into an oval. Fold each oval in half lengthwise. Pinch the seams to seal, and tuck ends under. Place in pans seam side down. Cover and let rise in a warm draft-free place for 60–90 minutes or until doubled in bulk.

About 30 minutes before the rise is completed, preheat oven to 350°. Bake approximately 45 minutes until golden brown on top and the loaf sounds hollow when tapped on the bottom. Remove from pans and let cool for one hour before slicing.

Yield: 2 loaves

NO-KNEAD BREAD

3 cups all-purpose or bread flour, plus more flour or cornmeal for dusting
¼ teaspoon instant or rapid-rise yeast
1½ teaspoons salt
Water
Cornmeal as needed
Optional: 2 tablespoons caraway seeds or rosemary, 3 tablespoons chopped olives, chopped onions, chopped walnuts, or anything else you imagine

In a large bowl combine flour, yeast, and salt. Add 1 ⅝ cups tepid water and stir until blended. Dough will be shaggy. Mix in the caraway seeds, chopped olives, onions, cheese, rosemary, walnuts or whatever additional ingredient you like. Cover bowl with plastic wrap. Let dough rest at least 12 hours, preferably 18, at warm room temperature. A turned-off oven provides a draft-free environment.

Dough is ready when its surface is dotted with bubbles. Lightly flour work surface and place dough on it. Sprinkle dough with a little more flour and fold it over on itself once or twice. Cover loosely with plastic wrap and let it rest 15 minutes.

Using just enough flour to keep dough from sticking to work surface or fingers, gently and quickly shape dough into a ball. Place a towel (not terry-cloth) or Silpat™ on a cookie sheet without sides. Generously coat towel or Silpat™ with flour or cornmeal; put dough seam side down on towel and dust with more flour or cornmeal. Cover with another cotton towel and let rise at room temperature for another 2 hours. When it is ready, dough will be more than double in size. If you poke it with a finger, the dent will remain.

At least one-half hour before dough is ready, heat oven to 450°. You will need a 6- to 8-quart heavy covered pot for a large "low-rise" loaf, or a 3- to 5-quart heavy covered pot for a smaller "hi-rise" loaf. Use cast iron, Pyrex™, or ceramic. If using Le Creuset™, the handle can withstand oven heat only up to 400°, so you will have to use another pot top. Put the pot into the oven as it heats. When dough is ready carefully remove pot from oven. Turn dough over into pot, seam side up. The dough may look like a mess, but shake the pan once or twice and it will straighten out as it bakes. Cover pot with lid and bake 30 minutes. Remove lid and bake another 15–30 minutes until loaf is beautifully brown. Cool on rack for at least one hour. It will be tempting to cut into it immediately.

Yield: 1½-pound loaf

Note: A covered cast iron pot is good for baking this bread.

PINEAPPLE-BANANA BREAD

2 cups flour
2 teaspoons baking powder
1 teaspoon baking soda
½ teaspoon salt
1 8¼-ounce can crushed pineapple, undrained
1 cup mashed bananas
⅓ cup orange juice
½ cup butter
1 cup sugar
2 eggs
1 cup chopped nuts

Preheat oven to 350°.

Sift flour with the baking powder, soda, and salt. Combine the pineapple, bananas and orange juice. Cream butter and sugar well. Add eggs, one at a time, beating well after each. Add flour mixture alternately with the fruits, mixing only enough to moisten the dry ingredients. Stir in the nuts.

Pour into a greased 9" x 5" loaf pan and bake for 1¼ hours or until done.

Yield: 1 loaf

RAY'S LEMON BREAD

2 cups all-purpose flour
1½ teaspoons baking powder
¾ teaspoon salt
1½ cups sugar
¾ cup corn oil
3 large eggs
3 tablespoons grated lemon peel
¾ cup finely chopped walnuts
¾ cup milk

Glaze:
½ cup fresh lemon juice
¼ cup powdered sugar

Heat oven to 350°. Butter and flour two 4" x 8" loaf pans.

Sift flour, baking powder and salt into a bowl. Combine sugar, oil, eggs and lemon peel in mixer bowl and beat for 2 minutes. Stir in nuts. Mix in dry ingredients alternating with milk in two batches, ending with dry ingredients. Divide the batter between the 2 loaf pans. Bake 1–1¼ hours until tester comes out clean.

Prepare glaze by stirring lemon juice with sugar until dissolved.

Run small knife around the loaves in pans to loosen. Brush glaze over hot breads allowing glaze to run down the sides. Cool completely and then turn out the loaves.

Can be prepared 2 days ahead. Wrap tightly and refrigerate.

Yield: 2 loaves

TROPICAL MUFFINS

½ cup sugar
1 egg
¼ cup milk
⅔ cup Grapenuts flakes
1 8-ounce can crushed pineapple, drained, reserving 2 tablespoons liquid for glaze
1 medium banana, thoroughly mashed
2 cups biscuit mix (Bisquick™)
½ teaspoon salt

Glaze:
1 cup powdered sugar
2 tablespoons reserved pineapple juice

Preheat oven to 425°.

Combine sugar, egg, and milk. Mix well. Add cereal, undrained pineapple, mashed banana, biscuit mix and salt. Stir until blended but not smooth. Spoon into greased muffin tins, filling ¾ full. Bake 20 minutes.

Mix powdered sugar with 2 tablespoons reserved pineapple juice until smooth to make the glaze. Remove muffins from pan and while they are hot, spread glaze on tops.

Yield: 1 dozen muffins or 4 dozen mini-muffins

CRANBERRY ORANGE MUFFINS

1 cup fresh or frozen cranberries, halved
½ cup sugar
1 egg
1 cup milk
2 tablespoons melted shortening
1 tablespoon grated orange rind
2 cups flour
3 teaspoons baking powder
2 tablespoons sugar
1 teaspoon salt

Preheat oven to 400°.

Combine the cranberries and the ½ cup sugar and set aside. Combine remaining ingredients in a large bowl. As soon as ingredients are moistened, stir in cranberries. Pour into greased muffin tins or tins lined with paper, filling them ⅔ full.
Bake 20–25 minutes.

Yield: 24 muffins

EASY ROLLS

1 package buttermilk biscuit dough, serving 8
¼ pound butter, melted
½ cup sesame seeds

Preheat oven to 375°.

Cut each biscuit into quarters. Pour melted butter into a 9" round cake pan. Sprinkle sesame seeds onto the butter. Place the biscuit quarters, top side down, onto the melted butter and seeds.

Bake according to package directions on biscuits, approximately 8–10 minutes. Break into pieces and serve.

Yield: 32 rolls

Note: Biscuit dough can be found in refrigerated cases of markets.

OATMEAL MUFFINS

⅔ cup milk
¼ cup oil
¼ cup molasses
¼ cup brown sugar
1 egg
1 cup whole wheat flour
1 cup oatmeal
1 tablespoon baking powder
¾ teaspoon cinnamon
¼ teaspoon salt
½ cup raisins

Preheat oven to 400°.

Combine all ingredients just until moistened. Divide batter evenly in a paper-lined muffin tin. Bake 15 minutes. Serve immediately.

Yield: 12 muffins

STREUSEL COFFEE CAKE

1 package dry yeast
1 cup sugar
1 cup milk, scalded and cooled to lukewarm
3 cups flour
6 ounces butter, plus 2 tablespoons
3 eggs

Preheat oven to 350°.

Make a sponge batter with yeast, 2 tablespoons sugar, milk, and 1 cup flour and blend well. Let rise until doubled in volume.

Cream 6 ounces butter and remaining sugar until light and fluffy. Add eggs one at a time and continue beating until well blended. Add sponge batter to butter and egg mixture and blend well.

Add remaining flour gradually. Grease three 8" or 9" cake pans. Divide dough
into 3 portions and place one in each pan. Melt remaining butter and brush over
dough. Let rise until double in bulk. Sprinkle streusel topping over dough. Bake
35–45 minutes.

Streusel topping:
⅓ cup flour
1 cup sugar
2 tablespoons butter, melted

Combine flour and sugar and mix well. Add melted butter gradually to dry ingredients, stirring with a fork. Continue mixing until mixture forms soft crumbly lumps.
Spread over top of dough after brushing with butter.

Yield: 3 cakes

LEMON-BASIL SHORTBREAD

1 cup butter, softened
½ cup sugar, plus 2 tablespoons for topping
1 teaspoon grated lemon zest
1 tablespoon lemon juice
2½ cups all-purpose flour
6 tablespoons cornstarch
1 tablespoon minced fresh basil leaves

Preheat oven to 300°.

In food processor, mix all ingredients, except 2 tablespoons sugar, until smooth.
Press dough into two 8" cake pans with removable rims. Press tines of a fork
around the edges to make a ridge pattern. Pierce dough with fork in parallel lines
about 1" apart. Bake until firm to the touch and lightly browned, about 45 minutes.

Sprinkle hot rounds with reserved sugar. Remove pan rims and cut each round,
while still warm, into 12–16 wedges. Let cool completely on pan bottoms on racks.
Remove wedges.

Wedges can be stored in an airtight container up to 1 week.

Yield: 24 or 32 wedges

ZUCCHINI-NUT MUFFINS

2 eggs
½ cup brown sugar, packed
½ cup honey
½ cup butter or margarine, melted
1 teaspoon vanilla
1¾ cups flour
1 teaspoon baking powder
1 teaspoon baking soda
1 teaspoon salt
1 teaspoon nutmeg
1½ teaspoons cinnamon
1 cup granola-type cereal
½ cup nuts, chopped
2 cups shredded zucchini

Preheat oven to 350°.

Beat eggs. Add brown sugar, honey, melted butter and vanilla. Beat well. Combine flour, baking powder, soda, salt, nutmeg, and cinnamon. Add to egg mixture and stir until just moistened. Stir in granola, nuts and zucchini.

Spoon into 18 greased or paper-lined muffin cups. Fill about ¾ full. Bake 25 minutes or until toothpick comes out clean. Serve warm or wrap and freeze.

Yield: 18 muffins

"I remember getting dressed up to go to Sunday lunches. That meant a dress for me and tie for Dyke. My mother wore a fur hat and gloves, and my dad wore a suit and a fedora. We parked in the driveway, and as we walked up the brick steps I felt excited to go inside. After greeting my grandmother, we went to the toy chest in the storage area, which was under the built-in seats in the inglenook, and played until lunchtime."
—MARGARET GAMBLE MESSLER WINSLOW

RITZ-CARLTON SCONES

1 cup butter at room temperature
1 cup powdered sugar
4 cups pastry flour
2 teaspoons baking powder
1 egg
1¼ cups milk
¼ teaspoon salt
¼ cup dried apricots, coarsely chopped
¼ pound raisins, chopped

Preheat oven to 400°.

Cream butter and sugar. Sift together flour and baking powder. Add to butter mixture. Mix in milk, salt and egg just to blend. Add chopped fruit. Use a tablespoon to drop dough into each section of a greased 4" muffin pan. Press each scone flat. Bake 8–10 minutes.

Yields: 4 dozen scones

Note: You can replace pastry flour with 1 tablespoon cornstarch, sifted with all-purpose flour and baking powder.

QUICK BUTTERMILK CORN BREAD

2 8½- ounce packages corn bread mix
1½ cups buttermilk
3 large eggs, beaten
¼ cup unsalted butter, melted

Preheat oven to 375°.

Butter a 9" x 13" x 2" metal baking pan. Combine corn bread mix with buttermilk, eggs and melted butter. Mix well and pour into prepared pan. Bake until a tester inserted into the center comes out clean, about 25 minutes.

Turn bread out onto a rack. Cool and wrap in foil if made a day ahead. Cut into squares.

Yield: 12 servings

BRUNCH

BAKED CROQUE MONSIEUR

16 ½" slices pain de mie or other fine-grained white bread
¼ cup Dijon-style mustard, optional
¾ pound sliced or grated cheese: Gruyere, Swiss, or cheddar
¾ pound sliced ham
1 medium-small onion, thinly sliced
6 large eggs
2½ cups whole milk
1 teaspoon herbes de Provence or mixed dried herbs of your choice
1 teaspoon salt

Topping
1½ cups panko (Japanese-style coarse breadcrumbs) or coarse homemade
   dried breadcrumbs
3 tablespoons butter, melted
¼ cup grated cheese: Parmesan, Gruyere, or cheddar

Butter a 9" x 13" baking pan. Remove crusts from the bread, if you wish. For firmer texture, toast the slices. Spread 8 slices of bread with mustard, if used. Place them into the greased baking dish, mustard side up, cutting slices as necessary, to cover the bottom of the pan completely. Top with half the cheese, ham, sliced onion, the remaining cheese, and the remaining bread. Press the sandwiches together with a spatula.

Beat the eggs, milk, and seasonings together. Pour slowly over the bread. Cover and place in the refrigerator for several hours or overnight.

About 1 hour before serving, preheat the oven to 400°. Mix panko with melted butter and grated cheese. Sprinkle over the sandwiches. Bake about 45 minutes, until the top is golden brown and the eggs set. Remove from the oven, and allow to rest for 10 minutes before cutting and serving.

Yield: 8–10 servings

"At Easter we hunted for Easter eggs which someone had hidden all over the terrace. I think we had ham for lunch on that occasion."
—MARGARET GAMBLE MESSLER WINSLOW

ASPARAGUS QUICHE

8 slices bacon
1½ pounds fresh asparagus
10 ounces Swiss cheese
2 tablespoons flour
2 eggs
¾ cup half-and-half
Salt and pepper
9" pie shell, partially baked and cooled

Preheat oven to 400°.

Fry bacon; drain and crumble.

Cut asparagus crosswise on the bias into 3 or 4 pieces. Steam until barely tender.

Grate the cheese and mix with the flour. Whisk the eggs with the half-and-half, salt and pepper. Add flour mixture. Sprinkle bacon in bottom of pie shell. Add asparagus and pour the cream mixture on top.

Bake for 40 minutes or until the center is firm.

Yield: 6–8 servings

Note: When adding asparagus, you can also add 10 sliced mushrooms.

CHICKEN-CRANBERRY HASH

2½ cups peeled, cooked, cold potatoes, cut into ½-inch dice
1½ cups diced, cooked chicken
1 cup thinly sliced green onions (white & green parts)
½ cup dried cranberries
⅓ cup half-and-half
1 teaspoon crumbled, dried sage leaves or 1 tablespoon fresh chopped sage
Salt and pepper to taste
2 tablespoons vegetable oil

Combine all ingredients in a large bowl and toss to blend well.

Heat oil in a large skillet over medium heat. Add mixture and spread to an even thickness. Cover skillet and cook for 15 minutes, stirring up bottom of hash every 5 minutes.

Uncover skillet, increase heat to high, and cook until hash is golden brown and crusty, stirring occasionally, about 10 minutes.

Yield: 4 servings

Note: Can be doubled, tripled or quadrupled and topped with poached eggs if desired.

BRUNCH STRATA

⅓ cup vegetable oil
3 cups sliced fresh mushrooms
3 cups chopped zucchini
2 cups fully cooked ham, cubed
1½ cups chopped onions
1½ cups chopped green peppers
2 garlic cloves, minced
2 8-ounce packages cream cheese, softened
½ cup half-and-half
12 eggs
4 cups day-old bread, cubed
3 cups (12 ounces) shredded cheddar cheese
1 teaspoon salt
½ teaspoon pepper

Preheat oven to 350°.

In a large skillet over medium-high heat, sauté the mushrooms, zucchini, ham, onions, green peppers and garlic in oil until vegetables are tender, but not browned. Drain and pat dry; set aside.

In a large mixing bowl, beat cream cheese and half-and-half until smooth. Beat in eggs. Stir in the bread, cheese, salt and pepper and vegetable mixture. Pour into two greased 11" x 7" x 2" baking dishes.

Bake uncovered for 35–40 minutes or until a knife inserted near the center comes out clean. Let stand for 10 minutes before serving.

Yield: 2 casseroles, 8 servings each

BELGIAN ENDIVE WITH HAM AND CHEESE SAUCE

8 endives (approximately 1 pound)
8 thin slices of ham
2 cups milk
2 bay leaves
10 peppercorns
Sprig of thyme
¼ cup butter
½ cup all-purpose flour
Salt, pepper, and nutmeg to taste
½ cup grated Gruyere cheese
½ cup grated cheddar cheese

Preheat oven to 450°.

Bring endives to a boil in salted water and simmer 8-10 minutes. Drain and wrap each with a slice of ham. Place in a shallow baking dish.

Bring milk, with bay leaves, peppercorns and thyme, to a boil in a saucepan and then cool.

In another saucepan, melt butter and whisk in flour. Cook over low heat and eliminate lumps. Strain milk and gradually add to butter, stirring until it thickens. Season with salt, pepper, and a dash of nutmeg. Add Gruyere cheese and mix well.

Pour sauce over endives and sprinkle with cheddar cheese. Bake for 10–15 minutes. Broil until cheese is brown and bubbling.

Yield: 8 servings

CHICKEN IN PASTRY

3 chicken breast halves, skinned and boned
1½ cups chicken broth
½ cup dry sherry
6 thin slices ham
Dijon mustard
2 tablespoons fresh tarragon or 2 teaspoons dried tarragon
6 thin slices Swiss cheese
6 frozen puff pastry shells, defrosted

Preheat oven to 400°.

Poach chicken breasts in broth and wine for 20 minutes. Cool in broth and cut each piece in half. Wrap each piece in ham. Spread with a thin coat of mustard. Sprinkle with tarragon and wrap in cheese.

Place puff pastry shells on a lightly floured surface and roll out each into a 4" circle.

Wrap one shell around each chicken breast and seal edges by wetting the dough. Place seam side down on an ungreased baking sheet, and bake for 20 minutes or until puffed and golden.

Yield: 6 servings

Note: This chicken dish can be baked just before leaving for a picnic. Covered loosely with foil, it will stay warm for several hours. Broth used for poaching chicken may be saved for another use.

FLORENTINE QUICHE

1 baked 9" pastry shell
1½ cups frozen spinach
4 tablespoons butter
Salt and freshly ground pepper
½ pound ricotta cheese
3 eggs, lightly beaten
½ cup freshly grated Parmesan
½ cup heavy cream or milk
Grated nutmeg to taste

Preheat oven to 375°.

Cook spinach with butter and salt and pepper to taste. Drain thoroughly and add remaining ingredients. Spread mixture in pre-baked pastry shell and bake for 30 minutes, or until custard has set.

Yield: 6 servings

Note: Freshly grated Parmesan is essential, but milk may be substituted for the cream with no noticeable difference.

HONEY ALMOND GRANOLA

4 cups old-fashioned rolled oats (not quick-cooking)
1 cup oat bran
2 cups whole almonds, coarsely chopped
¾ cup vegetable oil
¾ cup honey
1 tablespoon pure vanilla extract
½ teaspoon pure almond extract
1 cup nonfat dry milk powder
½ teaspoon table salt
1 cup cranberries, raisins, pepitas, pumpkin seeds or a combination, optional
Vegetable oil spray

Preheat oven to 325°. Spray two rimmed baking sheets with vegetable oil spray.

In a large bowl, mix the oats, oat bran, and almonds. In a small bowl, whisk together the oil, honey, vanilla, almond extract, dry milk powder, and salt. Pour the mixture over the oats and stir until well combined. Divide the mixture between the two oiled baking sheets and spread in an even layer. Bake for 20 minutes, stir, and bake another 10 minutes until the oats are golden brown and the nuts look well toasted. Don't overcook. Oats may feel soft but will be crunchy when cooled completely. If using dried fruit and nuts, add now.

Yield: Approximately 10 cups

Note: The granola will last about three weeks in an airtight container.

GREEN EGGS, NO HAM

I tablespoon olive oil
I bunch green onions, chopped
I bag washed spinach, coarsely chopped
5 eggs, beaten

Sauté the onion in olive oil. Add spinach and cook just until wilted. Add eggs and scramble all until eggs are done as desired.

Serve with whole grain toast and/or cantaloupe and white wine.

Yield: 2 servings

Note: This is fun to do with children. They can cut up the spinach with scissors and beat the eggs with a fork while you chop and sauté the onions.

CURRIED MUFFINS

I cup chopped ripe olives
½ cup chopped green onions
I ½ cups shredded cheddar cheese
½ cup mayonnaise
Salt to taste
I teaspoon curry powder
6 English muffins, split

Heat broiler to high.

Combine olives, green onions, cheese, mayonnaise, salt and curry powder. Mix well. Spoon onto muffin halves and broil until cheese melts. Serve immediately.

Yield: 12 pieces

SPINACH AND ONION FRITTATA

1 large onion, chopped
1 package frozen chopped spinach, thawed and squeezed dry
2 tablespoons butter, plus more for muffin pans or ramekins
10 eggs
½ cup grated Swiss cheese
¼ cup grated Parmesan cheese
¼ cup whipping cream
1 teaspoon paprika
1 teaspoon salt

Preheat oven to 325°.

Sauté onion and spinach in butter until onion is translucent. Set aside to cool. Beat eggs well in a large bowl and add all ingredients, mixing thoroughly.

Pour the batter into 12 well-buttered muffin pans or individual ramekins, filling ⅔ full. Bake for 20 minutes or until mixture is set.

Serve at room temperature.

Yield: 12 servings

GOLDEN SHRIMP CASSEROLE

8 slices day-old white or French bread
1 pound fresh sliced mushrooms
2 tablespoons melted butter
2 cups large cooked shrimp
3 large eggs
2 cups milk
½ cup sherry
½ pound sharp cheddar cheese, grated
¼ cup green onion, chopped
1 teaspoon dry mustard
1 teaspoon each salt, pepper, and paprika

Preheat oven to 300°.

Butter 9" x 13" Pyrex baking dish. Butter bread and cut in cubes. Sauté mushrooms in melted butter. Place alternate layers of bread, shrimp and mushrooms in baking dish.

Beat eggs with milk and sherry. Add remaining ingredients with ¾ of the cheese. Pour over the mixture in the baking dish and top with the remaining cheese.

Bake approximately 45–50 minutes or until knife inserted in the center comes out clean. Be careful not to overbake.

Yield: 6-8 servings

CHICKEN CURRY SALAD FOR A CROWD

Salad:
3 quarts cut-up chicken meat
2½ cups sliced celery
2½ cups pineapple chunks, drained
2½ cups slivered toasted almonds
2½ cups sliced water chestnuts
15 fresh, washed, and dried grape leaves or lettuce leaves
½ cup toasted, slivered almonds, optional

Dressing:
2 cups mayonnaise
1 cup sour cream
4 tablespoons lemon juice
3 tablespoons soy sauce
2 tablespoons curry powder or to taste
Lettuce or fresh grape leaves

Mix the salad ingredients. Mix together the remaining ingredients for the dressing. Mix salad and dressing. Refrigerate one hour or longer to let flavors blend. Serve on lettuce or grape leaves and garnish with seedless green grapes, parsley, and a few toasted almonds on top.

Yield: 15 servings

Note: Curry powder varies in heat, so be sure to use sparingly at first and taste dressing while mixing. A little paprika may be added if desired.

ENTRÉES

OVEN-ROASTED BRANZINO WITH HAZELNUT CRUMBS

Olive oil
2 slices hearty country white bread (about 2 ounces)
20 hazelnuts, shelled, roasted, peeled, and chopped
I clove garlic, minced
I teaspoon chopped mint leaves
I teaspoon orange zest
4 whole branzino, scaled and cleaned, about 2 pounds (black sea bass or farmed
   striped bass may be substituted)
Salt and freshly ground black pepper
I lemon, cut into 8 quarter-inch slices

Heat ½ cup olive oil in small sauté pan and sauté bread until golden. Remove bread and let cool, then crush into crumbs.

In a medium bowl, place bread crumbs, hazelnuts, garlic, mint, orange zest, and ½ teaspoon olive oil and mix thoroughly. Taste and adjust seasoning, then let sit for at least I hour to let flavors develop.

When almost ready to serve, preheat oven to 400°. Season fish with salt and pepper and stuff cavities of each fish with 2 lemon slices. Coat fish with olive oil and arrange on oiled pan. Roast in oven for 7 minutes on each side or until done. Sprinkle hazelnut crumbs on top of each fish to serve.

Yield: 4 servings

HALIBUT WITH FENNEL SAUCE

2 cups loosely packed fennel fronds, preferably wild
¼ teaspoon chopped garlic
½ cup olive oil, plus 4 tablespoons
⅛ teaspoon salt, plus extra for seasoning fish
⅜ teaspoon fresh lemon juice, or more to taste
4 6-ounce halibut steaks
Freshly ground black pepper

Place rack close to broiler flame and preheat broiler to high.

Blanch the fennel greens in boiling water for about 15–20 seconds. Drain. Purée the fennel in a blender with the garlic, then drizzle ½ cup olive oil into the blender with ⅛ teaspoon salt and add lemon juice to taste.

Brush both sides of each fillet with remaining olive oil and season with salt and fresh pepper. Place on broiler-proof pan and broil for 5 minutes on each side, or until done. Spoon 2 tablespoons of fennel sauce on each fillet and serve immediately.

Yield: 4 servings

BAKED FISH WITH TOMATOES AND HERBS

4 lean white fish fillets (about 1 pound) such as sole or orange roughy
2 tablespoons plus 2 teaspoons lemon juice, divided
½ teaspoon paprika
1 cup finely chopped seeded tomatoes (or 1 cup canned, diced tomatoes, drained)
2 tablespoons capers, rinsed and drained
2 tablespoons finely chopped fresh Italian parsley
1½ teaspoons fresh or dried basil
2 teaspoons olive oil
¼ teaspoon salt

Preheat oven to 350°.

Coat 12" x 8" baking dish with cooking spray or lightly coat with olive oil.

Arrange fish fillets in pan; drizzle 2 tablespoons lemon juice over fillets. Sprinkle with paprika. Cover with foil.

Bake for 18 minutes or until opaque in the center and the fish flakes easily when touched with a fork.

Meanwhile, in a saucepan, mix tomatoes, capers, parsley, the remaining 2 teaspoons of lemon juice, basil, oil, and salt.

Five minutes before the fish is done, place the saucepan over high heat.

Bring tomato mixture to a boil. Reduce heat and simmer for 2 minutes or until bubbling hot. Serve fish topped with tomato mixture. Additional parsley or basil may be added for garnish.

Yield: 4 servings

FLOUNDER WITH NORMANDY SAUCE

1 whole flounder or turbot (approximately 1 pound), cleaned
7 tablespoons butter, plus extra for baking dish
Salt and pepper
1¼ cups dry white wine, divided
2 teaspoons flour
30 live mussels, scrubbed
12 button mushrooms
2 tablespoons lemon juice
3 egg yolks
¼ cup heavy cream

Put the flounder in a generously buttered ovenproof dish. Season the fish, pour in 1 cup of the wine and put the dish in a preheated 350° oven for about 20 minutes or until the fish is cooked.

Put 2 tablespoons of butter in a saucepan and, over medium heat, stir in the flour until the mixture becomes golden. Moisten this with butter and wine from the fish, leaving in the dish only enough liquid to ensure that the fish does not dry up. Reduce the sauce mixture by half.

Put the mussels in another saucepan with the remaining ¼ cup of wine, cover and shake over high heat until all the shells have opened. Poach the mushrooms for 2–3 minutes in a little water with lemon juice, 1 tablespoon of butter, and a pinch of salt.

Beat egg yolks and cream together and set aside. Add the strained juices from the mussels and the mushrooms to the sauce. Over medium high heat reduce the mixture by half, then whisk in the egg yolk and cream mixture.

Arrange the mussels and mushrooms around the fish and pour the sauce on top. Dot the dish with the remaining butter, cut into small pieces. Put the fish in the oven for 2 minutes to reheat before serving.

Yield: 4–6 servings

SEA BASS EN PAPILLOTE

1 pound sea bass, cut into 4-6 portions
Juice of 1 large lemon or lime
Salt and pepper
2 tablespoons olive oil
½ onion, julienned
½ bell pepper, julienned
2 teaspoons chopped garlic
1 teaspoon fresh oregano, chopped
1-2 medium tomatoes, coarsely chopped
Foil or parchment paper
Butter for parchment paper
¼ cup sliced green olives
1 tablespoon capers
½ cup white wine

Preheat oven to 350°.

Sprinkle fish with lemon or lime, salt and pepper and set aside.

Heat olive oil over medium heat and sweat onion, pepper, garlic, oregano, and tomatoes in olive oil until just softened. Do not brown. Simmer until most liquid is evaporated. Remove from heat.

Cut filets into individual portions, place on squares of foil or buttered parchment paper. Top filets with sauce, olives, and capers. Divide wine among packages. Seal edges. Bake 10–12 minutes.

Serve packet on plate. Cut an "X" across top of packet and peel back to release steam and aroma.

Yield: 4–6 servings

SALMON WITH PEAS

1 large onion, sliced very thinly
1½ cups cold water
6 tablespoons olive oil
1½ teaspoons salt
⅛ teaspoon freshly ground pepper
3 pounds small fresh peas (about 3 cups) or 2 10-ounce packages frozen tiny peas
6 salmon steaks about ½ pound each

Place onion in a skillet with 1½ cups water, oil, salt and pepper. Bring to a boil; then simmer, covered, for about 10 minutes or until the onion is soft.

Add salmon steaks and simmer covered for 5 minutes. Add peas and continue cooking until fish easily flakes from the bones.

Yield: 6 servings

SCALLOPS IN HERB BUTTER

1 pound frozen bay scallops, thawed
3 tablespoons butter
2 shallots, peeled and finely chopped
2 cloves garlic, peeled and finely chopped
2 tablespoons chopped parsley
1 tablespoon fresh basil or 1 teaspoon dried basil
Pepper to taste

Preheat oven to 425°.

Drain scallops and divide among four 1-cup ramekins or custard cups.

Melt butter in a small pan and cook shallots for 2 minutes. Cool. Add garlic, parsley, basil, salt and pepper. Spoon mixture over scallops and cover with foil. Bake approximately 12–14 minutes.

Yield: 4 servings

FRICASSEE OF SEA SCALLOPS

1 pound sea scallops, rinsed and muscle removed
All-purpose flour, for dusting
Salt and pepper to taste
¼ cup oil
4 tablespoons cold butter, diced, plus 4 tablespoons for sautéing
¾ cup finely diced leeks
½ cup white wine
2 teaspoons minced garlic
½ cup fish stock
1 ear of corn, kernels scraped with a sharp knife into a bowl
¾ cup tomato, coarsely chopped
½ cup fresh basil, finely cut into julienne

Pat scallops dry after cleaning. Dredge the scallops lightly in flour seasoned with salt and pepper.

Heat a large sauté pan until hot. Add 2 tablespoons butter and cook until scallops are lightly browned on one side (3–5 minutes).

Turn scallops and sauté about 2 minutes more until lightly browned on both sides. Remove scallops to drain on paper towels.

Discard the cooking oil in sauté pan, but do not wash the pan. Working quickly, add 2 tablespoons butter to the pan over moderately high heat. When the butter sizzles, add the leek and sauté for 1 minute.

Deglaze pan with white wine. Add garlic. Reduce liquid by half.

Add stock and simmer 1 minute. Add the corn and tomatoes. Cook for 2 minutes. Remove pan from heat. Whisk in 4 tablespoons butter one tablespoon at a time and finish with salt and pepper. Add julienne of basil.

Divide the sauce among six warmed plates. Arrange scallops on sauce and serve.

Yield: 6 servings

INDONESIAN SHRIMP AND CORN

4 ears corn, husked
1 tablespoon olive oil
1 tablespoon sesame oil
⅔ cup plus 2 tablespoons chopped red onion
½ teaspoon minced garlic
½ teaspoon minced ginger
¼ teaspoon crushed red pepper flakes, or more to taste
1 tablespoon red wine vinegar (not balsamic)
¼ cup light brown sugar, packed
2 tablespoons soy sauce
1¼ cups smooth peanut butter
¼ cup ketchup
2 tablespoons dry sherry
4 tablespoons fresh lime juice
2 tablespoons basil chiffonade
1 pound shrimp, peeled and deveined
2 cups sliced celery
½ teaspoon minced jalapeño pepper, more to taste

Over a high flame or under the broiler, grill corn on all sides until some of the kernels become blackened. When cool, scrape kernels into a large mixing bowl.

Cook olive oil, sesame oil, red onion, garlic, ginger, and red pepper flakes in a small heavy-bottomed pot on medium heat until the onion is transparent, 10–15 minutes. Whisk in the vinegar, sugar, soy sauce, peanut butter, ketchup, sherry, and half of the lime juice. Cook for one more minute and add to corn.

Bring to a boil 3 quarts of water (add seasonings if you want) and add shrimp. Return to a boil and cook for about 1–2 minutes until done. Plunge shrimp immediately into ice water to stop the cooking. Drain. Cut each shrimp in half and add to the corn mixture. Add remaining onion, celery, and jalapeño pepper. Toss until mixed. Chill for 2 hours.

Add remaining lime juice and basil just before serving and toss again lightly.

Yield: 4 servings

CRAB CAKES

1½ cups panko or other coarse bread crumbs
3 tablespoons butter
¼ red bell pepper
1 stalk celery
5 green onions
1 16-ounce can fresh crabmeat
2 tablespoons mayonnaise
2 tablespoons lemon juice
1 egg, beaten
Salt and pepper, to taste
Seasoned salt, optional

Preheat oven to 350°.

Sauté 1¼ cup panko in 2 tablespoons butter until light brown. Season with seasoned salt, if desired. Chop bell pepper, celery and onions, and sauté in remaining butter until soft. Cool.

Combine remaining panko, sautéed vegetables, crab, mayonnaise, lemon juice, egg, and salt and pepper.

Form into 10 balls and roll in browned crumbs. Place on greased cookie sheet. Flatten slightly. Cover and refrigerate for at least 1 hour. Bake 20–30 minutes. Serve with fresh tartar sauce.

Tartar Sauce:

1 tablespoon finely chopped dill pickles
1 tablespoon finely chopped capers
1 teaspoon minced parsley
1 teaspoon grated white onion
1 cup mayonnaise

Mix all ingredients well. Keep chilled until ready to use.

Yield: 5 servings

Note: Panko can be found in Asian supermarkets and some other markets.

25-MINUTE BOUILLABAISSE

12 mussels
12 small clams, such as littleneck or Manila
½ cup very hot tap water
1 teaspoon saffron threads
¼ cup extra virgin olive oil, plus extra for croutons
1 medium onion, halved lengthwise, cut into thin slices
1 clove garlic, minced
1 tablespoon orange zest, 2" long and ⅛" wide
4 sprigs fresh parsley
1 cup dry white wine
1 28-ounce can Italian-style plum tomatoes with juice or 3 pounds ripe tomatoes,
  cored and quartered
8 large uncooked shrimp, peeled with tail on
12 ounces assorted firm white fish such as monkfish, halibut, or cod,
  cut into 1½" pieces

Optional:
4 half-inch slices French or Italian bread brushed with olive oil and toasted
  until golden, as croutons.

"I vividly remember my grandmother served crudité platters, olives, and at each place the best salted almonds in little silver dishes lined with cobalt blue glass. My favorite dish was peppermint-stick ice cream with hot fudge sauce. My least favorite was sweet potatoes with the marshmallows on top. I would try to just scrape off the marshmallows so I didn't have to eat those yucky orange sweet potatoes."

—TRACY GAMBLE HIRREL

Place shellfish in large bowl and rinse with several changes of cold water. Pull beard from mussels. Return to bowl. Cover with moist paper towel and refrigerate until ready to cook.

Mix hot water and saffron in small bowl. Cover and let stand until ready to use.

In a large broad saucepan with a tight-fitting lid, heat olive oil over medium-low heat and add onion and garlic, stirring occasionally until onion is translucent, about 5 minutes. Add orange zest and parsley.

Add wine and bring mixture to a boil over high heat. Add tomatoes and return to a boil, breaking up tomatoes with sides of a spoon. Add saffron threads and soaking liquid. Simmer uncovered over low heat for 10 minutes. (Can be prepared ahead up to this point and refrigerated. Bring broth to a boil before continuing.)

Arrange mussels and clams in single layer in simmering broth. Add shrimp and pieces of fish. Cover and cook over medium-high heat until mussels and clams are open and seafood is cooked through, about 3–5 minutes. Do not overcook.

If using croutons, place one in bottom of each of 4 shallow soup bowls. Divide fish and seafood evenly and divide broth among soup plates.

Yield: 4 servings

ITALIAN MEAT PIE

1 tablespoon vegetable oil
1½ pounds ground beef
1 cup prepared meatless spaghetti sauce
½ cup chopped bell pepper
½ cup chopped onion
6-8 mushrooms, sliced
½ cup sliced black olives, pitted
½ teaspoon Italian seasoning
Salt and pepper to taste
1 unbaked 9-inch pie shell
1 cup grated mozzarella cheese
½ cup grated Parmesan cheese

Preheat oven to 350°.

Brown beef in the oil and drain thoroughly. Add sauce, pepper, onion, mushrooms, olives and seasonings. Simmer 15 minutes.

Layer bottom of pie shell with ⅓ cup of mozzarella. Spread half the meat mixture on top. Sprinkle ⅓ cup of Parmesan over this. Spread remaining meat mixture and top with remaining mozzarella and Parmesan. Bake for 30 minutes. Slice into wedges and serve.

Yield: 4–6 servings

ENCHILADA PIE

2 pounds lean ground beef
¼ cup oil
2 large onions, chopped
4–5 garlic cloves, minced
Salt and pepper to taste
1 tablespoon oregano
½ teaspoon chili powder
¼–½ tablespoon crushed dried red pepper
1 7-ounce can diced green chili
1 19-ounce can hot enchilada sauce
2 4-ounce cans chopped ripe olives
½ pound mushrooms
1 pound cheddar cheese, grated
12 corn tortillas

Preheat oven to 350°.

Sauté onions in oil over medium heat until limp. Add the beef and garlic and brown. Add remaining ingredients except grated cheese and tortillas. Mix well.

Tear the tortillas into pieces. Layer tortilla pieces in a 2-quart casserole. Add meat mixture and grated cheese, layering 2 or 3 times, ending with cheese on top. Cover and bake about 45 minutes.

Yield: 8 servings

STEAK PIZZAIOLA

2 pounds beef steak (round or rump roast) cut into ¼" steaks, patted dry
¼ cup extra virgin olive oil
2 cloves garlic, chopped
1 small onion, thinly sliced
2 cups canned tomatoes, drained & chopped (or premium jarred marinara sauce)
Salt and pepper
1 teaspoon dried oregano or 1 tablespoon fresh oregano
½ cup red wine, optional

Pound steak until ⅛" thick.

Put oil, garlic and onion in frying pan and cook over medium heat until golden brown. Remove garlic and onion with spoon and save. Increase heat and brown meat, 1–2 minutes on each side. Do not crowd steaks. Remove meat when brown and place on warm platter.

Return garlic and onion to pan, add tomatoes, salt and pepper and wine. Cook and simmer rapidly, until oil and tomatoes separate, about 15 minutes. Stir in oregano.

Return steaks to pan and cook for another 5 minutes.

Yield: 6–8 servings

BEEF STEW

2 pounds chuck or round beef, boned
⅓ cup flour
1 tablespoon oil
1–2 onions, chopped
2 teaspoons salt
1 tablespoon sweet Hungarian paprika
1 tablespoon cider or tarragon vinegar
1½ teaspoon caraway seeds
1 teaspoon marjoram
1 teaspoon capers
2 bay leaves
Parsley sprigs
⅔ cup dry sherry

Pat beef dry with paper towels and cut beef into 1½" cubes. Dredge well with flour. Heat oil in a 3½-quart Dutch oven over medium high heat and brown meat on all sides. Add onions, seasonings, and liquid. Cover and cook over very low heat for about 1½ hours or until meat is very tender. Remove bay leaves and parsley.

Yield: 4 servings

LAMB SHANKS

¼ cup flour, or more as needed
Salt and pepper
½ teaspoon dried oregano
6 lamb shanks, each cut into 4 pieces crosswise (ask butcher to do this)
⅓–½ cup olive oil
¾ cup chopped onions
¾ cup chopped celery
¾ cup peeled carrots, chopped
2–3 large cloves garlic, minced
¾ cup Cabernet, Zinfandel, Merlot or any dry red wine
1 bouillon cube, dissolved in 8 ounces of water

Preheat oven to 350°.

While heating oil in a large heavy skillet over medium heat, mix flour, oregano, salt, and pepper in a paper bag. Shake 3 or 4 pieces of lamb shanks at a time in the flour mixture. When each piece is thoroughly dredged, brown in oil and transfer to large casserole. Repeat until all pieces are browned. Reserve flour mixture.

Sprinkle vegetables, including garlic, over lamb.

Add wine and bouillon to skillet and cook over high heat, stirring constantly, for 3 minutes. Pour into casserole. Cover and bake until lamb is tender, about 2 hours. Remove from oven.

In a small cup mix 1–2 teaspoons of remaining flour mixture with 4 tablespoons cold water. Add to casserole, stirring for a few minutes until thickened.

Yield: 6 servings

BUTTERFLIED LEG OF LAMB

1 5–6 pound leg of lamb, boned and butterflied
Fresh mint leaves, bruised
1 cup olive oil
2 cloves garlic, minced
2–3 lemons, juiced
¾ cups red wine
Coarsely ground pepper

Blend all ingredients except lamb into a marinade. Marinate lamb 2 hours or more.

Grill over hot coals as for steak for 45 minutes, turning once or twice. From time to time baste with marinade.

Slice on the bias.

Yield: 6–8 servings

"Lunchtime was very much the same each week, the same food and routines. My grandmother sat at the head of the table nearest the kitchen, and my grandfather at the end nearest the porch. We filed into the dining room and went to our assigned seats where a glass of tomato juice was waiting, but first someone said grace. Sometimes we would have hot tomato soup, which would be served after we had all been seated. In front of each place setting always stood a small, cobalt blue-lined silver dish with salted almonds. We could nibble on these while waiting to be served. Children were expected to be polite and mannerly and quiet."

—MARGARET GAMBLE MESSLER WINSLOW

ROASTED PORK LOIN WITH LEEKS

3 large leeks, about 2¼ pounds
½ cup water
1 tablespoon butter, divided
½ teaspoon salt, divided
½ teaspoon ground black pepper, divided
2-pound boneless pork loin, trimmed
½ cup dry white wine
Chopped fresh parsley, optional

Remove roots and tough outer leaves from leeks. Cut each leek in half lengthwise. Cut each half crosswise into ½" slices. Soak in cold water to loosen dirt. Drain, rinse and drain again.

Combine leeks, ½ cup water, 1 teaspoon butter, ¼ teaspoon salt, and ¼ teaspoon pepper in a Dutch oven large enough to hold the loins. Cook over medium-high heat for 10 minutes until leeks wilt. Pour the leek mixture into a bowl and set aside.

Heat remaining butter in Dutch oven over medium-high heat. Brown pork on all sides, about 5 minutes. Add remaining salt, pepper, and wine to pan, cooking 15 seconds to scrape brown bits from bottom of pan. Return leek mixture to pan, cover and simmer about 2 hours or until tender. Remove pork from Dutch oven and place on heated serving platter. Increase heat to high to reduce leek sauce. Cut pork into ¼" thick slices. Serve with leek mixture. Garnish with parsley, if desired.

Yield: 4–6 servings

ROASTED PORK LOIN

2 pounds pork loin roast
1 clove garlic, slivered
Salt and pepper to taste
2 tablespoons melted butter
1 cup dry white wine
1 cup apple sauce
1 large apple, peeled, cored and cut into thin slices
3 tablespoons brown sugar
½ cup heavy cream

Preheat oven to 450°.

Wipe the pork dry and cut slits in the meat with a sharp knife and insert the garlic slivers. Rub the roast with salt and pepper.

Place fat side up in a roasting pan and roast in oven for 30 minutes. Mix the butter and wine with the fat in the pan and continue to roast the pork for another 30 minutes, basting with pan mixture 2–3 times. Reduce heat to 350° and continue to roast the pork for 1 hour longer, basting with pan drippings every 10 minutes.

Remove the pan from the oven. Pour off ¾ of the pan drippings. Spread the apple-sauce over the meat. Sprinkle the apple slices with brown sugar and arrange slices around the roast. Return pan to the oven, basting the apple slices with pan juices until they are tender, about 10 minutes. Add cream to the pan and let it cook with the apples and pan juice for 5 minutes.

Remove pan from the oven, slice the pork and serve on a warmed platter with the apples and pan juices.

Yield: 6 servings

GRILLED PORK CHOPS
WITH BASIL-POMEGRANATE SAUCE

6 pork chops, about 1" thick
Salt
Pepper
½ cup pomegranate molasses
¼ cup water
1 clove garlic, crushed
2 tablespoons minced fresh basil, plus additional for garnish
1 tablespoon canola oil

Wipe pork chops dry and season with salt and pepper. Set aside.

Put pomegranate molasses, water, garlic, and basil in a small saucepan. Bring to a boil and turn heat to low. Simmer for 5 minutes. Remove from heat and add salt and pepper to taste. Strain into gravy boat. The sauce can be made earlier and reheated.

Pour oil into a large cast iron skillet and heat over high heat until oil begins to shimmer. Add pork chops and sear for 2 minutes, then turn and sear the other side. Reduce heat to medium and cook for about 4 minutes on one side. Turn chops again and cook for another 4 minutes or until desired doneness.

Place on serving platter or individual dishes, garnish with remaining basil and serve with pomegranate sauce.

Yield: 6 servings
Note: Pomegranate molasses is found in Middle Eastern markets.

SPICED PORK CHOPS WITH MANGO AND MINT SALSA

¾ teaspoon chili powder
¼ teaspoon salt
⅛ teaspoon ground allspice
4 boneless, center cut pork loin chops, trimmed
Cooking spray
1½ cups peeled, finely chopped mango
2 tablespoons chopped, fresh mint
½ teaspoon grated lemon rind
1 tablespoon fresh lemon juice
2 teaspoons sugar
¼ teaspoon crushed red pepper

Combine first three ingredients and sprinkle evenly over pork chops. Coat a large nonstick skillet with cooking spray over medium-high heat. Add pork and cook for 4 minutes on each side, or until done.

Combine mango, mint, lemon zest and juice, sugar, and pepper in a medium bowl and serve with pork.

Yield: 4 servings

50-CLOVE GARLIC CHICKEN

8–10 chicken thighs
2 teaspoons salt
¼ teaspoon pepper, plus additional to taste
Pinch nutmeg
3 tablespoons olive oil
50 whole garlic cloves, peeled
4 stalks celery, cut into ½" slices, including the tops
6 sprigs parsley
1 tablespoon dried tarragon
Pumpernickel or sourdough bread

Preheat oven to 375°.

Sprinkle chicken with salt, pepper and nutmeg. Brown in oil to give it some color. Add to a 3-quart casserole along with the garlic, celery, more pepper, nutmeg and the herbs. Tightly cover the pot with foil and place the lid on top. Bake 1½ hours. Do not remove lid while baking.

Serve in the casserole along with some pumpernickel or sourdough bread. Put some of the oil and the soft garlic cloves on slices of bread as a spread.

Yields: 4 servings

"My grandfather was a little austere but always ready to share his passion for birds. He had parakeets and canaries and bred them, keeping dozens in cages outside. There was always music from canaries singing and chatter from the parakeets. As you walked into the dining room, in the far right corner, there was a cage with one or two yellow canaries. They warbled throughout the meal."

—MARGARET GAMBLE MESSLER WINSLOW

BAKED CHICKEN WITH HERBS

4 chicken breast halves, boned
¼ cup melted butter
1½ pounds fresh spinach, stems removed
2 cups plus 1 tablespoon white wine
2 cups chicken stock
2 shallots, finely sliced
2 cups whipping cream
6 fresh tarragon sprigs, plus additional for garnish
6–7 fresh basil leaves
Salt and pepper

Preheat oven to 375°.

Place chicken in baking dish with melted butter, turning to coat pieces.

Bake 25–30 minutes or until done.

Meanwhile wash spinach leaves and pat dry with paper towels.

Combine the chicken stock, 2 cups white wine, and shallots in a saucepan or skillet. Bring to boil over medium heat and boil until liquid is reduced by one fourth. Stir in cream and simmer until sauce thickens to consistency that will coat a wooden spoon, about 10 minutes.

Remove chicken from baking dish, discard fat, and deglaze dish over high heat with 1 tablespoon of white wine, being sure to scrape and include brown bits.

Add cream sauce and blend.

Drop spinach leaves, tarragon, and basil into sauce. Bring to boil and simmer briefly, stirring gently. Add salt and pepper to taste. Gently remove spinach from sauce and divide into 4 mounds on serving platter or onto individual dinner plates.

Remove skin from chicken breasts. Place each piece of chicken on a spinach mound.

Remove tarragon and spoon sauce over the chicken. Garnish with additional tarragon.

Yield: 4 servings

CHICKEN ARTICHOKE CASSEROLE

2 whole chicken breasts, halved
1 teaspoon salt, divided
½ small onion, sliced thin
9 ounces frozen artichoke hearts
½ pound fresh mushrooms, sliced
2 tablespoons butter
¼ cup flour
¼ cup butter

¾ teaspoon white pepper
1¾ cups half-and-half
½ cup Parmesan cheese, grated
½ teaspoon dried, crumbled rosemary

Preheat oven to 325°.

In a pan, bring 2 cups of water, 1 teaspoon salt, and the onion to a boil. Lower heat and poach chicken breasts until tender. Cool, skin, remove meat from the bone and cut into large pieces. Prepare artichoke hearts according to package directions. Drain. Melt 2 tablespoons butter in skillet and sauté mushrooms until tender. Drain and set aside. In the same skillet or small saucepan melt ¼ cup butter. Stir in flour, remaining salt and pepper and cook briefly. Add half-and-half. Cook, stirring constantly, until thickened. Do not boil. Stir in Parmesan cheese and rosemary.

Place chicken in a 7" x 11" baking dish. Cover with artichokes. Spread the sauce over top and sprinkle with mushrooms. Bake 30 minutes.

Yield: 4 servings

MARMALADE CHICKEN

4 chicken breasts, halved, boned and skinned
½ cup red currant jelly
1 cup orange marmalade
1 tablespoon soy sauce
1 8-ounce can sliced water chestnuts, drained
1 11-ounce can mandarin oranges

Preheat oven to 350°.

Place chicken pieces in greased baking dish.

Mix well the jelly, marmalade, soy sauce, and syrup from the oranges. Add the water chestnuts and orange segments. Spoon over chicken and bake uncovered for 40 minutes. Baste with pan juices. Cover and cook an additional 20 minutes or until done.

Chicken may be served alone or over steamed rice. Apricot-pineapple preserves may be substituted for the marmalade.

Yield: 8 servings

GINGER CHICKEN

Sauce:
½ cup orange juice
¼ cup lemon juice
3 tablespoons soy sauce
1 tablespoon honey
½ cup chicken stock
½ cup dry sherry

Combine juices, soy sauce, honey, chicken stock and sherry. Heat to simmering. Set aside.

Chicken:

⅛ teaspoon pepper
1 teaspoon salt
½ cup flour
3 pounds chicken breasts, skinned, boned and halved
1 tablespoon powdered ginger or 2 teaspoons grated fresh ginger
½ cup oil

Preheat oven to 300°.

Combine pepper, salt, flour, and ginger. Coat chicken pieces in flour mixture. Brown coated chicken in hot oil. Arrange chicken in baking pan. Cover with sauce and bake 1 hour.

Yield: 6 servings

INDIAN SPICED CHICKEN

2 chickens, cut up (about 6 pounds)
1 clove garlic, minced
3 tablespoons lemon juice
1 tablespoon ground coriander (or less)
1 teaspoon each ground cumin and turmeric
½ teaspoon ground ginger
¼ teaspoon each ground mace, cloves, cinnamon, nutmeg, salt and pepper
¼ cup oil
Chutney

Preheat oven to 425°.

Arrange chicken pieces skin side up in large pan—do not crowd. Place garlic in small bowl and add remaining ingredients, except chutney. Blend well. Spread spice mixture on chicken with fingers or a pastry brush. Any leftover mixture can be put on underside of chicken. Cover loosely with foil and refrigerate until 1 hour before cooking. Remove foil and bake for 45 minutes. Skin should be crisp and brown. Serve with chutney.

Yield: 6 servings

Note: This dish should be baked at least 4 hours before serving to enhance flavors. It can be prepared 1–2 days in advance and warmed in a 250° oven.

PERSIAN CHICKEN

Oil for casserole
4 skinned and boned chicken breasts
1 8-ounce carton plain yogurt
1 tablespoon lemon juice
1 tablespoon soy sauce
¾ teaspoon ground coriander
⅛ teaspoon curry powder
⅛ teaspoon fresh ground black pepper
¼ cup sliced almonds

Lightly oil a 10" x 6" casserole.

Mix all the ingredients except the chicken and nuts in the casserole. Add chicken to the casserole, turning it to coat it thoroughly. Cover and marinate several hours in the refrigerator. Bring the casserole to room temperature for one hour.

Preheat oven to 375°.

Bake uncovered for 1 hour. Baste 2 or 3 times during the last half hour, adding almonds during last 10 minutes.

Yield: 4 servings

PISTACHIO CHICKEN

Oil for baking dish
4 chicken breasts, halved, skinned and boned
½ cup pistachio nuts, finely chopped
⅓ cup lemon juice
½ cup butter, melted
¾ cup dry white wine
½ teaspoon chopped cilantro
½ teaspoon paprika

Preheat oven to 350°.

Cut a pocket in each of the halves of chicken and fill with 1 tablespoon of the nuts. Put in greased 9" x 13" baking dish. Mix remaining ingredients and pour over the chicken.

Bake uncovered for 40 minutes. Baste with the pan juices, cover and continue to cook until done, about 10–20 minutes more.

Yield: 8 servings

HERBED CORNISH GAME HENS

3 Cornish game hens (if frozen, allow to thaw in refrigerator overnight)
6 sprigs fresh rosemary, plus more for garnish if desired or 1 tablespoon
  dried rosemary
Salt and pepper
⅓ cup olive oil
⅓ cup lemon juice
5 large cloves garlic, minced or pressed
2 tablespoons fresh thyme leaves, or ¾ teaspoon dried thyme
Bay leaf, crumbled
½ cup butter
Watercress for garnish

Use kitchen scissors to cut each bird along backbone from neck to tail or ask butcher. In 2 flat dishes, place a sprig of fresh rosemary under each half bird, or sprinkle underside with dried crumbled rosemary.

Prepare marinade with remaining ingredients except butter and pour over hens. Cover with plastic wrap and refrigerate at least 2 hours or overnight.

Preheat broiler to high.

Transfer birds to platter, reserving rosemary sprigs and marinade. Place rosemary sprigs on shallow broiler-proof pan large enough to hold the 6 hen pieces. Pat birds dry with paper towels. Brush on all sides with melted butter, salt, and pepper. Place hens skin side down and broil for 10 minutes, basting every 3–5 minutes with reserved marinade.

Turn hens skin side up, with rosemary sprigs on top, and continue to baste, broiling for another 10–15 minutes.

Discard charred rosemary and transfer birds to warm platter. Garnish with watercress or additional fresh rosemary.

Yield: 6 servings

CATALINA JALAPEÑO CORNISH HENS

3 Cornish game hens, split, or 6 boneless chicken breast halves
1 8-ounce jar jalapeño jelly
2 oranges
1 red bell pepper
1 green bell pepper

Preheat oven to 350°.

Place chicken or hens skin side up in an oven-proof pan sprayed with non-stick cooking spray. Cut unpeeled oranges and bell peppers into wedges and place around chicken. Spread jalapeño jelly over all, covering well. Cover pan and bake for 45 minutes. Uncover, baste with pan juices, and bake an additional 25–30 minutes or until nicely browned.

Yield: 6 servings

YELLOW CHILI

1 onion, chopped
2 yellow bell peppers, coarsely chopped
3 yellow squash, sliced and the slices quartered
1 12-ounce can whole kernel corn
3 tablespoons olive oil
1 teaspoon whole cumin (or ½ teaspoon ground)
1 teaspoon chili powder
½ teaspoon seasoned salt
Tabasco sauce to taste
1 15-ounce can kidney beans
1 15-ounce can pinto beans
1 15-ounce can chili beans
½ pound fresh baby carrots, cut in chunks
3 chicken breasts coarsely ground, or 1½ pounds ground chicken or turkey
1 tablespoon ground cardamom

Sauté onion, yellow pepper, squash, and corn in 2 tablespoons olive oil. Add cumin, chili powder, seasoned salt, Tabasco, undrained beans, and carrots. Bring to a boil, reduce heat and simmer ½ hour.

Sauté chicken in remaining 1 tablespoon olive oil. Add cardamom and cook 10 minutes. Add to chili mixture and simmer 10 minutes. Adjust seasonings.

Yield: 8-10 servings

Note: Omit chicken for a vegetarian dish.

ORIENTAL CHICKEN WINGS

10–20 chicken wings
⅓ cup soy sauce
⅓ cup brown sugar
⅓ cup butter, melted

Preheat oven to 375°.

Rinse wings in cold water. Dry with paper towels.

Cut wings into 3 sections, discarding the tips. Place pieces in a baking pan.

Mix remaining ingredients in a small sauce pan. Heat until well blended and pour over chicken wings. Bake until sticky, about 40 minutes.

Yield: 6 servings

FLORENTINE CHEESE CASSEROLE

2 small bunches spinach, washed thoroughly, or 1 box frozen chopped spinach, thawed, drained, and squeezed dry
3 eggs
1 cup cottage cheese
2 tablespoons chopped onion
2 teaspoons Worcestershire sauce
1 scant teaspoon salt
½ pound grated cheddar cheese
2½ cups cooked brown rice
3 tablespoons melted margarine or butter

Preheat oven to 350°.

Cook fresh spinach briefly until wilted. Squeeze dry in clean dish towel. Beat the eggs and stir in the cottage cheese, onion, salt and cheese. Fold in the spinach, rice and margarine. Turn into greased 1-quart baking dish. Bake 20–30 minutes.

Yield: 4 servings

EGGPLANT CASSEROLE

1 eggplant, about 1½ pounds
¼ cup salad oil
1 15-ounce can tomato sauce
1 4-ounce can chopped green chiles
½ cup green onions, thinly sliced
½ teaspoon cumin
½ teaspoon garlic salt
1 2¼-ounce can sliced ripe olives, drained
1½ cups cheddar cheese, grated
Sour cream

Preheat oven to 450°.

Cut unpeeled eggplant in ½" slices, brush both sides with oil. Place on baking sheet and bake until soft, about 20 minutes.

In a sauce pan combine remaining ingredients except cheese and sour cream. Simmer, uncovered, for 10 minutes.

Make a single layer of the eggplant slices in the bottom of a shallow 1½-quart casserole. Spoon over half the sauce and sprinkle with half the cheese. Repeat the layering, ending with cheese. Bake, uncovered, at 350° until bubbling, about 25 minutes.

Garnish individual servings with sour cream, as desired. For a milder sauce, use half the amount of chiles.

Yield: 6 servings

SPINACH LASAGNE

1 pound ricotta
1½ cups shredded mozzarella, divided
1 egg
1 10-ounce package frozen chopped spinach thawed and drained
½ teaspoon salt
¾ teaspoon oregano
⅛ teaspoon pepper
1 32-ounce jar spaghetti sauce (with or without mushrooms, peppers, etc.)
8 ounces (approximately) uncooked lasagna noodles
1 cup boiling water
Grated Parmesan or Romano cheese, optional
Butter or oil for pan

Preheat oven to 350°.

Mix ricotta, 1 cup mozzarella, egg, spinach, salt, pepper, and oregano together.

In greased 9" x 13" pan, layer ½ cup sauce, ⅓ of uncooked noodles and half the cheese mixture. Repeat layers, top with remaining noodles, then rest of sauce. Sprinkle with remaining ½ cup mozzarella. Cover tightly with foil. Refrigerate overnight.

Lift one corner of foil and pour in boiling water at corner. Re-cover corner tightly. Bake for 1 hour and 15 minutes. Let stand 15–20 minutes before cutting into servings.

Top each serving with grated Parmesan, Romano, or a combination of the two, if desired.

Yield: 8-12 servings

Note: For a low calorie version, replace ricotta with non-fat cottage cheese, and mozzarella with 1 pound diced firm tofu (tofu absorbs the flavor of the sauce).

RATATOUILLE

2 cups yellow or zucchini squash in ½" cubes
2 cloves garlic, minced
3 medium tomatoes, diced
2 cups peeled, diced eggplant
3 medium onions, sliced
½ teaspoon dill seed
¼ teaspoon oregano
Salt and pepper to taste
2 green peppers, sliced
2 tablespoons oil

Preheat oven to 350°.

Layer vegetables and sprinkle with herbs and seasonings. Pour oil over all and bake for 45–60 minutes. Serve hot or at room temperature.

Yield: 8 servings

TOFU WITH MIXED VEGETABLES

1 14-ounce package firm tofu
1 8-ounce package frozen mixed vegetables
2 tablespoons sesame oil
2 tablespoons soy sauce
1 tablespoon sugar

Drain and cut tofu into four pieces. Place tofu onto a microwave-safe plate.

Arrange mixed vegetables around tofu.

Mix sesame oil, soy sauce, and sugar in a small bowl. Pour sauce over tofu and vegetables.

Cover plate tightly with plastic wrap. Place plate on a rack (such as a bacon rack) on a turntable.

Microwave on high for 10–15 minutes.

Yield: 4 servings

SIDES

ACORN SQUASH WITH APPLES

2 acorn squash
2 large apples, peeled, cored and diced
2 teaspoons honey
2 teaspoons lemon juice
3 tablespoons chopped walnuts, optional
½ teaspoon ground cinnamon, optional
¼ cup raisins, optional
¼ cup apple or orange juice

Preheat oven to 350°.

Halve squash and remove seeds. Bake, cut-side down, in ¼" water for 30 minutes. Combine remaining ingredients. Fill squash halves with mixture and bake, cut-sides up, for an additional 30 minutes. If browning too quickly, cover loosely with aluminum foil.

Yield: 4 servings

APRICOT-CRANBERRY SAUCE

1 12-ounce package cranberries
2 cups sugar
1 cup dried apricots, cut into ½" pieces
1 cup golden raisins
1 cup water
1 cup orange juice
1 tablespoon grated orange zest

Combine all ingredients. Stir over medium heat until sugar dissolves and cranberries pop. Cool and refrigerate. It will thicken as it cools. Can be made 1–2 days in advance.

Yield: 5 cups

ANNIE'S BARLEY WITH ORANGE AND DATES

3 tablespoons unsalted butter
1 small white or yellow onion, finely chopped
5 or 6 dates, pitted and chopped
Finely grated zest of 1 orange
1 cup pearl barley
3 cups chicken or vegetable stock, or water
Kosher salt
5 or 6 sprigs of fresh thyme, leaves only, minced
½ small bay leaf
Freshly ground black pepper

In a medium nonstick saucepan, melt the butter over medium-high heat. Add the onion and cook until soft, about 5 minutes. Add the dates and orange zest and sauté for a minute or two longer. Add the barley and stir to coat with the butter. Pour in the stock and add 1 teaspoon salt, the thyme, and bay leaf. Bring to a boil, reduce the heat so that the liquid simmers, cover, and cook until the barley is tender and the liquid has been absorbed, about 30–40 minutes. Remove from heat and let sit covered for 5–10 minutes. Remove the bay leaf, season with pepper, fluff with a fork, and serve.

Variations: use lemon zest instead of orange zest. You can also mix in cooked or grilled chicken, beef or lamb for a main dish.

Yield: 4–6 servings

Note: The barley will keep for about two weeks in the refrigerator. It can be reheated in a baking dish in the oven. Dot the top with butter, cover with aluminum foil and bake at 350° for 20 minutes or until warmed through.

ASPARAGUS À LA POLONAISE

⅓ cup butter
⅓ cup soft bread cubes
2 hard cooked eggs, chopped
1 tablespoon chopped parsley
Salt and pepper to taste
2 pounds fresh asparagus, parboiled

Melt butter until foamy. Stir in bread cubes. Cook over low heat until crisp and golden. Remove from heat. Add eggs, parsley and seasonings and stir to combine. Serve over asparagus.

Yield: 4 servings

ASPARAGUS WITH TOMATILLOS

1 pound asparagus
3 tablespoons olive oil
4 large tomatillos, husked, cored and finely diced
1 small Roma tomato, cored and finely diced
Salt and pepper to taste
¼ cup finely shredded Parmesan cheese
Lemon wedges

Trim asparagus and cook in 1" of water until just tender, 3–5 minutes. Drain and immerse in ice water. When cool, drain and arrange equally on four salad plates, or on one large platter. Mix oil, tomatillos and tomato. Season with salt and pepper. Spoon over asparagus. Sprinkle with cheese. Garnish with lemon wedges.

Yield: 4 servings

GARLIC-BRAISED BROCCOLI RABE

1 pound broccoli rabe, trimmed and cut into 1" pieces
2 tablespoons olive oil
2 garlic cloves, sliced
Freshly ground black pepper
Salt

Microwave broccoli rabe in a covered dish for 2 minutes until barely cooked. Heat olive oil in a large skillet over medium heat. Add garlic and sauté until lightly browned. Add broccoli rabe, salt, and pepper. Sauté about 2 minutes.

Yield: 8 servings

GRADUATION DINNER BRUSSELS SPROUTS

¼ cup toasted pine nuts
24 Brussels sprouts
8 shallots
¼ cup extra virgin olive oil
2 tablespoons salted butter
Kosher salt and cracked pepper to taste

Toast pine nuts in large skillet over medium heat until light brown. Stir constantly with spatula and do not let the pine nuts burn. When pine nuts are golden brown, remove from heat and set aside.

Clean Brussels sprouts and remove any tough outer leaves and any stems. Cut each sprout in half and slice each half in slices. Slice shallots in same fashion.

Over medium heat in the same large skillet, heat butter and extra-virgin olive oil. Add sprouts and shallots and mix. The mixture needs to be slightly caramelized and soft to the bite, cooked about 20 minutes. Add kosher salt and cracked pepper to taste. Remove from heat, toss with toasted pine nuts and serve.

Yield: 6–8 servings

SWEET AND SOUR CABBAGE

¼ cup butter
½ cup chopped onion
I large red cabbage, shredded (8 cups)
½ cup sugar
I tablespoon lemon juice
½ cup cider vinegar
I tablespoon salt
¼ teaspoon pepper
¼ teaspoon caraway seeds

In a large skillet, over medium high heat, sauté onion in butter until golden, about 5 minutes. Add remaining ingredients, mix well. Cook, covered, over medium heat about 20 minutes or until cabbage is tender.

Yield: 6-8 servings

VANILLA CARROTS

16 baby carrots (real baby carrots from a farmers' market), or very small, slender carrots
2 vanilla beans
3 tablespoons salted butter

Wash and peel carrots, leaving ½" green sprout on each carrot. Soften vanilla beans in warm water until tender and pliable. Dry vanilla beans and with a knife make a slit down the length of the bean. With the tip of the knife remove as many vanilla seeds as possible. Sauté whole carrots in butter until tender, coat carrots with vanilla seeds and cook I minute longer. Serve two to each person.

Yield: 8 servings

Note: Save remaining vanilla pieces in a jar with I pound sugar to make vanilla sugar.

CHORIZO, SQUASH AND JALAPEÑO CORN BREAD STUFFING

1 small butternut squash, peeled and cut into ½" cubes (2 cups)
½ cup water
Salt
12 ounces chorizo, casing removed
½ cup (1 stick) butter
1 large onion, chopped
2 cups chopped green onions (about 8 large)
1 cup chopped celery
½ cup coarsely chopped seeded deveined jalapeños (about 4)
1 cup chopped fresh cilantro
1 tablespoon chopped fresh sage, or 1 teaspoon dried
1 box buttermilk cornbread mix
4 large eggs
½ cup (or more) low-salt chicken broth

Combine squash and ½ cup water in large, heavy skillet; bring to boil over medium-high heat. Cover; reduce heat to medium. Cook until squash is almost tender, about 7 minutes. Uncover; sprinkle with salt. Boil uncovered until squash is tender and water has evaporated, about 2 minutes longer. Cool completely.

Sauté chorizo in large, heavy skillet over medium-high heat until cooked through and fat is rendered, breaking up chorizo with back of fork, about 5 minutes. Transfer chorizo and drippings to strainer set over bowl. Melt butter in same skillet over medium-high heat. Add onion, green onions, celery, and chilies. Sauté 8 minutes. Mix in drained chorizo, cilantro, sage, and squash. (Can be made 1 day ahead. Cover and chill.)

Preheat oven to 350°.

Butter 13" x 9" x 2" glass baking dish. Coarsely crumble corn bread mix into extra-large bowl. Add chorizo mixture. Beat eggs and ⅓ cup broth in small bowl. Add to stuffing; toss gently, mixing in more broth by ¼ cupfuls if dry. Transfer stuffing to prepared dish. Cover with buttered foil, buttered side down. Bake 45 minutes. Uncover and bake until top of stuffing is crisp and golden, about 15 minutes.

Yield: 12 servings

JALAPEÑO CHEESE CAULIFLOWER

3 cups lightly cooked cauliflower florets, placed in shallow 2-quart baking dish
1½ tablespoon butter, melted
1 tablespoon flour
¾ cup milk
¾ cup jalapeño jack cheese, diced or grated

Preheat oven to 350°.

In a saucepan over medium heat, melt butter and add flour, stirring constantly for 3 minutes. Add milk and continue to stir until well blended. Add cheese and stir until melted. Pour over cauliflower and bake for 15 minutes.

Yield: 4-6 servings

COLCANNON

2 cups hot, mashed potatoes
4 tablespoons butter, plus extra if desired
1 small onion, finely chopped
2 cups finely chopped cabbage (parboiled 20 minutes)
¼ cup chopped parsley, optional

Heat butter in a large skillet and sauté onion for 5–7 minutes until soft and translucent, but not brown. Add drained cabbage and stir over low heat for 2 minutes. Fold in mashed potatoes. Serve hot, topped with a knob of butter and garnished with some chopped parsley.

Potato mixture can also be formed into patties about 1" thick and 3–4" in diameter and browned in a little additional butter.

Yield: 4 servings

CORN CASSEROLE

1 small box Jiffy corn bread mix
1 15-ounce can whole corn
1 15-ounce can creamed corn
1 cup sour cream
4 tablespoons melted butter
½ cup grated cheddar cheese
Chopped jalapeño peppers, optional

Preheat oven to 350°.

Mix first 5 ingredients together and place in a greased 9" x 9" pan. Top with grated cheese and sprinkle with jalapeño peppers. Bake for 40 minutes until cheese melts.

Yield: 8-10 servings

CREAMY COMPANY POTATOES

4 large russet potatoes, peeled and sliced ⅛" thick
2 cloves garlic, minced
3 cups milk
2 teaspoons salt
Black pepper
½ cup heavy cream
½ cup fresh chopped basil or 3 tablespoons dried
2 tablespoons butter

Preheat oven to 325°.

Butter a 9" x 13" casserole and rub with a cut garlic clove, then mince the garlic. In a large pot of water, bring the potatoes, chopped garlic, milk, salt, and pepper to a boil. Reduce heat and simmer for 10 minutes. Place mixture in casserole. Pour heavy cream over the potatoes and stir in basil. Mix well. Dot with butter. Bake uncovered for 1 hour.

Yield: 8–10 servings

SWEET POTATOES WITH TEQUILA AND LIME

1 ½ sticks butter or margarine, melted in pan
2 pounds sweet potatoes
2 tablespoons sugar
2 tablespoons tequila
1 tablespoon lime juice
Salt and pepper
Lime wedges

Peel sweet potatoes, then shred, using a food processor or coarse holes of a grater. Immediately mix with butter in pan, and sprinkle with sugar. Cook over medium heat until potatoes begin to caramelize and look slightly translucent, about 15 minutes, turning occasionally with a wide spatula.

Stir in tequila and lime juice. Cook, stirring, for 3 more minutes. Season to taste with salt and pepper. If made ahead, cover and refrigerate until next day. To serve, warm about 15 minutes over medium-low heat, stirring occasionally.

Pour sweet potatoes into a bowl. Garnish with lime.

Yield: 6–8 servings

"The main course on Sundays was roast chicken. On major holidays, my grandfather carved a turkey or ham at the table. Mildred brought the vegetables, mashed potatoes and gravy in a silver dish, and we served ourselves. Second portions were offered. Salad was often part of the meal. Then came dessert. Angel food cake with peppermint-stick ice cream was a favorite. So too was vanilla ice cream served with chocolate sauce. Mildred appeared from around the corner with the hot chocolate sauce in a silver pitcher on a plate. The pitcher was eight inches tall with a long, narrow neck."

—MARGARET GAMBLE MESSLER WINSLOW

ITALIAN MASHED POTATOES

1 head Napa cabbage
6–8 shallots
2 large cloves garlic
⅛ cup extra virgin olive oil
2 tablespoons salted butter
1 recipe for mashed potatoes that serves 6–8

Wash Napa cabbage and dry. Slice cabbage in half lengthwise and then again into quarters. Chop head from one end to the other in medium to small slices. Chop shallots in small slices. Finely mince garlic cloves.

Melt butter and oil over medium heat. Add vegetables and stir to coat. Reduce heat to low and allow vegetables to caramelize until mixture is dark golden brown. Fold this mixture into your traditional mashed potato recipe.

Yield: 6–8 servings

Note: If your traditional recipe includes nutmeg, please omit.

STREUSEL-TOPPED SWEET POTATOES

6 medium sweet potatoes, peeled and cut into ¼" slices
1½ cups heavy cream
2 tablespoons unsalted butter, softened
2 tablespoons all purpose flour
¼ cup light brown sugar, packed

Boil sweet potato slices in salted water for 3 minutes. Drain.

Preheat oven to 375°.

Lightly butter a 9" x 13" baking dish. Lay sweet potatoes in slightly overlapping rows in prepared dish. Pour cream over potatoes. Work butter, flour and brown sugar with fingers until well-combined. Sprinkle mixture over top of potatoes. Bake until potatoes are tender and topping is browned, 30–40 minutes.

Yield: 8 servings

MUSHROOM LOAF

3 pounds assorted mushrooms, cleaned
3 medium onions (1 pound)
¾ cup dry sherry
¾ teaspoon dried thyme
1½ teaspoons salt
¾ teaspoon ground black pepper
1 cup fresh bread crumbs or ¾ cup matzo meal
½ cup flour
4 eggs
½ cup whipping cream
¾ cup white wine
2 tablespoons fresh tarragon or 3/4 teaspoon dried
6 tablespoons butter

Put mushrooms and onions in food processor and pulse until fine. Place in 13" skillet or 2 smaller skillets and add sherry, thyme, salt, and pepper. Cook over medium heat, stirring occasionally, until mixture is dry, about 45 minutes.

Transfer mixture to large bowl and stir in bread crumbs or matzo meal. Add eggs one at a time, mixing well after each addition. Stir in cream and half the fresh tarragon.

Preheat oven to 375°.

Pour mixture into greased, 2½-quart loaf pan or bundt mold. Cover with foil and place loaf pan in hot water bath in oven for 2 hours. Loaf is cooked when toothpick inserted into center comes out clean. Remove loaf from oven and from water bath and set aside. (At this point, when it is cooled, you can cover it in the pan and freeze it for 2–3 weeks. If you do this, thaw mixture overnight and warm it in a 250° oven for about 1 hour before serving.)

Pour wine into saucepan. If using dried tarragon, add now. Cook over medium heat until liquid is reduced by half. If using fresh tarragon, add remainder at this point. Remove from heat and whisk in butter. Set aside and keep warm.

Unmold loaf and cut into ½" slices either onto serving platter or on individual plates, and spoon sauce over one corner of slices. Wine and tarragon sauce may be omitted. Sprinkle with extra fresh tarragon, or a mixture of fresh tarragon and parsley, instead.

Yield: 16 slices

SWEETS

MICROWAVE APPLE BETTY

4 cups peeled, sliced green apples
1 tablespoon sugar
2 tablespoons lemon juice
½ cup flour
½ cup old-fashioned oats
⅔ cup packed brown sugar
1 teaspoon cinnamon
1 teaspoon nutmeg
⅓ cup butter
½ cup chopped nuts

Place sliced apples in a buttered 8" × 8" glass baking dish and sprinkle with sugar and lemon juice.

In a bowl, combine the dry ingredients, except nuts, and use a pastry blender to cut in the butter until mixture resembles oatmeal. Add nuts and mix well. Spread mixture over sliced apples. Cover with plastic wrap. Microwave 10 minutes on high setting. Uncover and let set 10 minutes. Serve with whipped cream or vanilla ice cream, if desired.

Yield: 4–6 servings

APPLE CRUMP

5–6 thinly sliced pippin apples
Lemon juice, ½ medium lemon
½ cup water
½ teaspoon cinnamon
1 cup brown sugar
½ cup cold butter, plus extra for greasing pan
½ cup flour
¼ teaspoon salt
1 cup Grape-Nuts

Preheat oven to 350°.

Fill a 9" x 9" buttered baking dish with the apples. Sprinkle lemon juice, water and cinnamon over the apples.

Mix the remaining ingredients together with a pastry blender. Cover apples with this mixture and bake uncovered for 1 hour. Serve with cream.

This dessert looks elegant served in sherbet glasses.

Yield: 6–8 servings

HONEY CRUST APPLES

¼ cup chopped dates
1¼ cups honey
2 tablespoons chopped pecans
2 teaspoons grated lemon zest
½ cup graham cracker crumbs
1 teaspoon ground cinnamon
6 baking apples
⅓ cup melted butter
1 cup crème fraiche

Preheat oven to 400°.

Combine dates, ¼ cup of the honey, the nuts and lemon zest. In a separate bowl mix the crumbs and cinnamon. Peel the top third of the apples, core them and brush with melted butter. Roll each apple in the crumb mixture and place in a 10" x 6" x 2" baking dish. Spoon the date mixture into the center of each apple. Pour the remaining butter and honey over and around the apples. Bake for 30 minutes or until done, basting every 10 minutes with the honey mixture. Chill and serve, topped with crème fraiche.

Yield: 6 servings

Note: If you prefer to make your own crème fraiche, mix 1 cup heavy cream with 1 tablespoon buttermilk in a sterile, glass jar. Cover tightly and let stand in a warm place until the cream has thickened and soured, about 24–28 hours, depending on the room temperature. Chill for two hours, then whip lightly for smoother texture before using.

CRANBERRY CLAFOUTI

2 cups cranberries
1 cup sugar or to taste
½ teaspoon cinnamon
½ cup chopped walnuts
2 large eggs, beaten
1 cup flour
¾ cup melted butter, plus extra for greasing pan

Preheat oven to 325°.

Put washed and drained cranberries in a greased 10" pie pan. Combine ⅓ cup sugar with cinnamon and walnuts and sprinkle over the fruit. Beat remaining sugar into the eggs along with the flour and butter. Pour batter over cranberries. Bake for 1 hour or until crust is nicely browned.

Yield: 8 servings

LEMON ANGEL CHARLOTTE

6 large eggs, separated
1½ cups sugar
1½ teaspoons lemon zest
¾ cup lemon juice
1 envelope unflavored gelatin, softened in ¼ cup cold water
1 pint heavy whipping cream
1 tablespoon almond extract
2 tablespoons powdered sugar
Small angel food cake or a package of ladyfingers torn into small pieces

Beat 6 egg yolks, gradually adding ¾ cup sugar, lemon zest, lemon juice, and salt. Cook mixture in double boiler stirring constantly until slightly thickened. Add softened gelatin. Mix and let cool.

Beat egg whites until thick. Add remaining sugar gradually, 2 tablespoons at a time, beating after each addition. Fold into lemon mixture.

Whip cream. Add almond extract and powdered sugar. Fold into lemon-egg mixture.

Layer with cake pieces in a large glass bowl. Refrigerate.

Yield: 8–10 servings

PUMPKIN CHIFFON PIE

3 egg yolks
½ cup sugar, divided in half
1¼ cups canned cooked pumpkin
½ cup milk
½ teaspoon salt
½ teaspoon ginger
½ teaspoon cinnamon
½ teaspoon nutmeg
1 tablespoon gelatin
¼ cup cold water
3 stiffly beaten egg whites
½ cup sugar
1 9" baked pastry shell, cooled
Whipped cream

Beat egg yolks and ¼ cup sugar until thick. Add pumpkin, milk, salt and spices. Cook in double boiler until thick. Remove mixture from heat.

Soften gelatin in cold water and add to the pumpkin mixture. Beat egg whites with remaining sugar and then add to pumpkin mixture.

Pour into cooled baked shell and chill. Top with a sprinkle of additional nutmeg.

Top with whipped cream when served.

Yield: 6–8 servings

LEMON-LIME CURD

5 large eggs
2 cups sugar
10 tablespoons butter, melted and cooled
Grated zest and juice of 3 lemons
Juice of 1 lime

Beat the eggs well, adding sugar gradually while beating. Slowly add the butter, then the lemon juice and zest. Put in top of double boiler over simmering water and cook, stirring constantly, until the curd thickens. Stir in lime juice. Cool and refrigerate.

Yield: 3 cups

Note: This keeps several weeks and is delicious on scones or biscuits or as a tart or cake filling. Warmed, it is a marvelous topping for gingerbread with a bit of whipped cream on top. This recipe does not double.

LEMON MOUSSE

3 large eggs, separated
½ cup sugar
2 lemons, juice and zest
Salt
½ cup heavy cream

Combine egg yolks and sugar and beat until thick. Stir in lemon zest and juice. Pour into top of a double boiler over simmering water and beat constantly with a wire whisk until mixture thickens, about 10 minutes. Remove from heat and pour into a large mixing bowl and let cool. Beat egg whites with a pinch of salt until they hold firm, shiny peaks. Fold whites into egg yolks and lemon mixture. Refrigerate 1 hour. Whip cream and fold into chilled mousse. Serve in stemmed glasses.

Yield: 4 servings

PINEAPPLE-COCONUT DESSERT

Crust:
1 cup butter, softened, plus extra for greasing pan
½ cup sugar
3 egg yolks
½ cup sour cream
2½ cups all-purpose flour
1 teaspoon baking powder

Filling:
3 tablespoons all-purpose flour
2 egg yolks
2 8-ounce cans crushed pineapple, undrained
1 teaspoon vanilla extract
2 cups shredded coconut

Topping:
5 egg whites
½ cup confectioners' sugar
1 teaspoon vanilla extract

Preheat oven to 350°.

In a large mixing bowl, cream butter and sugar. Add egg yolks and sour cream and mix well. Combine flour and baking powder and gradually add to creamed mixture. Press into greased 13" x 9" x 2" baking pan. Set aside.

In a small saucepan, combine flour, egg yolks and pineapple. Cook and stir over medium heat until mixture reaches 160° and coats the back of a metal spoon. Remove from heat and stir in vanilla. Mix in coconut. Pour over crust.

In a small mixing bowl, beat egg whites to soft peaks. Gradually add confectioners' sugar and vanilla. Spread over filling. Bake for 45 minutes or until golden brown. Cool on a wire rack for 1 hour. Store in refrigerator.

Yield: 16 servings

CHOCOLATE MOUSSE PIE WITH RASPBERRY SAUCE

Crust:
1 8½-ounce package chocolate wafers
4 tablespoons butter, softened
1 tablespoon instant coffee dissolved in 2 tablespoons hot water

Preheat oven to 325°.

Crush cookies. Blend with butter and dissolved coffee. Press mixture into bottom and a little up the sides of a 9" spring-form pan. Bake for 8–10 minutes. Cool.

Filling:
6 ounces semi-sweet chocolate
4 tablespoons Kahlua
2 large eggs
2 egg yolks
¼ cup sugar
1 cup heavy cream

Melt chocolate with Kahlua in double boiler over low heat. Cool slightly. In a blender or food processor, blend eggs, egg yolks and sugar. Add cream and then chocolate mixture. Pour into crumb crust. Chill.

Raspberry Sauce:
1 10-ounce package frozen raspberries, thawed
1–2 tablespoons Triple Sec
Sweetened whipped cream, optional

Puree raspberries in blender. Force through sieve. Stir in Triple Sec and refrigerate.

To serve, spoon 2–3 tablespoons of raspberry purée on serving dish. Place serving of mousse pie on puree. Top with sweetened whipped cream if desired.

Yield: 6–8 servings

MANGOES FLAMBÉ

1 large, ripe mango
Orange juice
¼ cup Cognac
¼ cup orange marmalade or apricot preserves
1 pint vanilla ice cream

Dice or slice the fruit into a rimmed dish, saving the juice. Drain juice into a measuring cup and add enough orange juice to make ¼ cup of liquid. Put fruit in heat-proof bowl. Warm the Cognac in small saucepan and ignite. Pour over the fruit. Combine the juice, marmalade and fruit. Serve over ice cream.

Yield: 4 servings

OZARK PUDDING

2 large eggs
1 cup sugar
4 tablespoons flour
2½ teaspoons baking powder
¼ teaspoon salt
1 cup chopped nuts
2 teaspoons vanilla
1 cup chopped apple
Whipped cream or ice cream
Butter for greasing pan

Preheat oven to 350°.

Beat eggs and sugar until smooth. Sift dry ingredients together and add to egg mixture. Add remaining ingredients except for whipped cream.

Pour into a buttered 9" square pan and bake for 40 minutes. Serve warm or at room temperature with whipped cream or ice cream.

Yield: 4 servings

SWEET ROSEMARY-PEAR PIZZA

Pastry:
2 cups all-purpose flour
¼ teaspoon salt
2 teaspoons sugar
10 ounces cold, unsalted butter, cut into chunks
1 large egg, beaten
3–4 tablespoons water
Oil for 14" or 16" pizza pan

Combine dry ingredients in a food processor. Cut in the butter with rapid pulses until it is the size of peas. Add the egg and 2 tablespoons water and pulse until the dough just starts to gather in clumps. Add a little water if too dry. Gather the dough from the processor and roll it into about a 17" circle. Oil pizza pan. Place dough on pan and drape extra dough back toward the center. Refrigerate for 30 minutes.

Topping:
1½ pounds firm, ripe Bosc Pears (4 or 5; others will also work if not too soft)
½ lemon or orange for juice
Zest of 1–2 oranges or lemons
1–2 teaspoons fresh rosemary leaves, finely chopped or ½–¾ teaspoon dried
1 teaspoon ground cinnamon
½ teaspoon ground black pepper
⅓ cup sugar
1 tablespoon basil leaves, shredded
2 tablespoons olive oil, optional
Shredded gorgonzola cheese, optional

Set oven rack to lowest position and heat oven to 500° for 30 minutes.

Core and cut each pear into about 14 vertical wedges (½" thick). Put slices in a bowl and drizzle lemon or orange juice over them.

Take dough from refrigerator. Fold the extra dough back over the pan edge. Arrange the pear slices in a spoke wheel pattern (very little overlap) starting at the rim of the pan, fat part of the pear toward the outside. Sprinkle with zest, rosemary, and olive oil. Fold extra dough over the fruit or make an edge.

In a small bowl, mix the zest, rosemary, cinnamon, pepper, sugar, and olive oil (if desired) with a fork. Sprinkle over the pears. Bake for 18–22 minutes until the edges of the crust are nicely browned. Sprinkle basil over the pizza after 10 minutes. If desired, add gorgonzola cheese after pizza is removed from oven. Serve hot, warm, or at room temperature.

Yield: 8 servings

TIRAMISU

8 large egg yolks
½ cup sugar
1½ pounds mascarpone
4 large egg whites, beaten to soft peaks
2 cups strong espresso coffee, cooled
½ cup brandy, optional
42 ladyfingers (crispy kind, not soft ones)
½ cup unsweetened cocoa powder
Semi-sweet chocolate bar for garnish

Beat egg yolks with sugar until thick and pale yellow. Fold the mascarpone into the egg yolk mix until very smooth, then fold in the egg whites.

Combine the espresso and brandy in a small bowl. One at a time quickly dip the ladyfingers into the liquid mixture and place them close together in the bottom of a 10" x 14" x 2" pan.

Evenly spread ½ of the mascarpone mix over ladyfingers. Put half the cocoa in a fine sieve and shake over pan. Repeat, dipping the remaining ladyfingers in the coffee/brandy mixture to make another layer. Add remaining mascarpone and then cocoa over the top. Cover with plastic wrap and refrigerate for several hours.

Make chocolate shavings with a vegetable peeler and sprinkle over tiramisu just before serving.

Yield: 10–12 servings

GREENE'S BIRTHDAY SPONGE CAKE

6, 8 or 10 eggs, depending on size
Sugar, sifted once before measuring
Flour, sifted once before measuring
½ teaspoon salt
2 teaspoons vanilla if using 10 eggs; reduce vanilla for fewer eggs

Preheat oven to 325°.

Weigh the eggs in the shell. For the sugar, weigh out the same amount as the eggs. For the flour, weigh out one-half the weight of the eggs. After arriving at the correct weight, sift flour and sugar separately three more times.

Separate egg yolks from whites and beat yolks. Gradually add the sugar to the yolks, beating until creamy. Add the vanilla.

Add the salt to the flour and with a spatula lightly fold the flour into the yolk mixture.

Whip egg whites until light and fluffy, but not dry. With a spatula fold whites into yolk mixture.

Pour batter into large ungreased tube pan and bake 60 minutes. Wooden pick inserted should come out clean. Invert on rack and cool.

This cake is good frosted with your favorite boiled frosting, or make an icing using powdered sugar, butter and lemon juice, adding grated lemon rind to taste.

Yield: 16–20 pieces

"This cake was a favorite birthday cake for years in the Henry Mather Greene family and was usually made by William Sumner Greene's grandmother, Charlotte A. Whitridge. I have tried many times by trial and error and perseverance to make the cake "taste like Nana's" and never could until I came up with this version. It has been quite a challenge!"

—HARRIOTT GREENE

CARROT-PINEAPPLE CAKE

1½ cups flour, plus extra for pan
1 cup sugar
1 teaspoon baking powder
1 teaspoon baking soda
1 teaspoon cinnamon
½ teaspoon salt
⅔ cup cooking oil
2 large eggs
1 cup grated raw carrots
½ cup crushed pineapple, with syrup
1 teaspoon vanilla
Butter for pan

Preheat oven to 350°.

Stir together dry ingredients in a large bowl. Add oil, eggs, carrots, pineapple and vanilla. Stir until all ingredients are moistened and then beat with an electric beater for 2 minutes at medium speed. Pour mixture into greased and lightly floured 9" x 9" x 2" cake pan. Bake about 35 minutes. Cool and frost in the pan with cream cheese pecan frosting.

Frosting:

1 3-ounce package whipped cream cheese
4 tablespoons butter, softened
1 tablespoon vanilla
2½ cups sifted powdered sugar
½ cup chopped pecans

Cream together the cheese and butter. Add the vanilla, and gradually add the sugar, blending well. Stir in the pecans.

Yield: 12 pieces

CHOCOLATE RUM CHEESECAKE

Crust:
18 chocolate graham cracker squares
¾ cup sugar
1 tablespoon unsalted butter at room temperature, plus extra for pan
1 large egg white

Adjust an oven rack to the center position and preheat oven to 350°. Butter an 8" springform pan and set aside.

Place graham crackers in a food processor and pulse until fine or put them in a zip-top plastic bag and crush them into fine crumbs with a rolling pin. In a medium bowl, beat together sugar, butter and egg white with an electric mixer for about 1 minute, until creamy. Add graham cracker crumbs and stir with a fork to moisten them thoroughly. Press crumbs into the bottom of the buttered pan and about 1¼" up the sides. Bake for 10 minutes. If the crust puffs up during baking, carefully tamp it down after removing the pan from the oven. Set aside on a cooling rack. Reduce the heat to 300°.

Filling:

3 ounces (3 squares) semisweet chocolate
3 tablespoons dark rum
¼ cup chocolate syrup
¼ teaspoon salt
1 teaspoon pure vanilla extract
2 large eggs
2 8-ounce packages Neufchatel cheese, at room temperature
1 cup sugar
2 tablespoons Dutch-process cocoa

For the filling, combine chocolate and rum in the top of a double boiler or in a small saucepan placed in a larger saucepan of hot water set over medium heat. Stir occasionally with a small wire whisk until chocolate is melted and the mixture is smooth. Remove pan from the water bath and whisk in chocolate syrup. Set aside.

In a large bowl, beat Neufchatel cheese with an electric mixer on medium speed until smooth, about 1 minute. Add sugar, cocoa, salt, and vanilla and beat until smooth, 1–2 minutes. On low speed, beat in melted chocolate mixture. Scrape the bowl and beat for another 30 seconds. On medium speed, add eggs one at a time, beating only until each is thoroughly incorporated, 20–30 seconds.

Scrape the batter into the cooled crust and lay a square of aluminum foil, shiny side up, loosely over the top of the pan. Bake for 45 minutes.

Turn the oven off, remove the foil, and leave cheesecake in the oven with door closed for another 45 minutes. Remove from oven and let cool to room temperature on a wire rack, then cover loosely with a paper towel and refrigerate for at least 8 hours, or overnight.

To serve, run a small, sharp knife around the edges of the cake and carefully remove the pan sides. Rinse a knife in hot water and shake off the excess before making each cut.

Yield: 8–10 servings

LEMON JELLO™ CAKE

1 package lemon Jello™
⅔ cup oil
1 box yellow cake mix
1 teaspoon lemon flavoring
4 large eggs
Butter and flour for greasing cake pan

Topping:
2 cups sifted powdered sugar
5 tablespoons softened butter
Juice of 1½ lemons

Preheat oven to 350°.

Dissolve lemon Jello™ in ¾ cup boiling water and cool. Mix Jello™ with ⅔ cup oil. Add cake mix and 1 teaspoon lemon flavoring. Blend and beat 4 minutes at medium speed. Add eggs, one at a time, beating after each addition. Pour into a buttered and floured 13" x 9" x 2" cake pan. Bake for 30 minutes.

Beat topping ingredients until well blended and of pouring consistency. Pour topping over hot cake when removed from oven.

Yield: 12–16 pieces

CHOCOLATE ZUCCHINI CAKE

½ cup butter, softened, plus extra for pan
½ cup vegetable oil
1¾ cups sugar
2 large eggs
1 teaspoon vanilla
2½ cups flour
¼ cup unsweetened powdered cocoa
1 teaspoon baking soda
½ teaspoon baking powder
½ teaspoon ground cinnamon
½ teaspoon ground cloves
½ cup buttermilk
2 cups shredded, peeled zucchini (about 3 medium)

Frosting:
1 cup flaked coconut
⅔ cup packed brown sugar
¼ cup milk
6 tablespoons butter, softened
½ cup chopped walnuts

Preheat oven to 325°.

In a large mixing bowl, beat butter, oil and sugar until smooth. Add eggs, one at a time, beating well after each addition. Beat in vanilla. Combine flour, cocoa, baking soda, baking powder, cinnamon, and cloves. To the butter and egg mixture add dry ingredients alternating with the buttermilk and ending with the flour mixture. Fold in zucchini.

Pour into greased 13" x 9" x 2" baking pan. Bake for 45–50 minutes until toothpick inserted in the center comes out clean. Cool on a wire rack for 10 minutes.

Preheat broiler. Combine frosting ingredients and spread over the warm cake. Broil 4–6 minutes until golden brown. Cool completely.

Yield: 12–16 servings

RED VELVET CAKE

3 tablespoons cocoa
2 ounces red food coloring
1 teaspoon vanilla
2 large eggs, lightly beaten
½ cup butter or margarine, softened, plus extra for pan
1½ cups sugar
½ teaspoon salt
2½ cups sifted cake flour, plus extra for pan
1 cup buttermilk
1 teaspoon baking soda
1 tablespoon vinegar

Preheat oven to 350°.

Make a paste of the cocoa, food coloring, and vanilla. Add beaten eggs. Cream butter or margarine and sugar. Add to egg mixture.

Mix salt with flour. Add flour mixture alternately with buttermilk, ending with flour.

Dissolve baking soda in vinegar and fold into cake mixture.

Divide batter evenly between two 9" layer pans that have been greased and floured lightly.

Bake for 25–30 minutes until cake tests done.

Fluffy White Frosting:
1 cup milk
5 tablespoons flour
Salt
½ cup butter, softened
½ cup shortening
1 cup confectioners' sugar
2 teaspoons vanilla

Cook milk, flour and salt over low heat until thick, stirring constantly. Cool to luke-warm. Cream butter, shortening, sugar, salt and vanilla. Add to flour and milk paste.

Whip at high speed with electric mixer until light and fluffy. Frost between layers, top and sides.

Yield: 8–10 servings

FUDGE COOKIES

2 tablespoons butter
1½ cups semi-sweet chocolate chips
1 can sweetened condensed milk
1 cup flour
1 cup chopped nuts
1 teaspoon vanilla

Preheat oven to 325°.

Melt the butter and chocolate chips in heated condensed milk. Add remaining ingredients. Drop by teaspoon onto greased cookie sheet. Bake for 15 minutes. Cool on racks.

Yield: 5 dozen cookies

CHOCOLATE PUDDING CAKE

1 cup flour
2 teaspoons baking powder
½ teaspoon salt
¾ cup sugar
2 tablespoons unsweetened cocoa
½ cup milk
1 egg
1 teaspoon vanilla
2 tablespoons melted butter, plus extra for pan
¾ cups coarsely chopped walnuts, optional
¾ cup brown sugar
¼ cup unsweetened cocoa powder
1¾ cups hot water

Preheat oven to 350°.

Mix together the first five ingredients with a wire whisk. Add milk and egg, mixing well. Add vanilla and melted butter. Stir in walnuts.

Pour the batter into a buttered (or vegetable oil-sprayed) 4-cup or 6-cup soufflé dish, or use an 8" square pan.

Mix brown sugar and cocoa together. Sprinkle on top of batter. Pour hot water over batter using a spoon to diffuse while pouring.

Bake for 45 minutes. Cake will be on top; sauce will be on the bottom.

Yield: 12 pieces

FLOURLESS ORANGE CAKE

Butter for greasing pan
Matzo cake meal or flour for dusting
2 thin-skinned juice oranges
1½ cups blanched almonds
1 cup sugar
6 large eggs, separated
Confectioners' sugar, optional

Preheat oven to 350°.

Butter a 10" springform pan and dust with matzo cake meal or flour.

Scrub oranges well and place in pot with water to cover. Cook, covered, over medium heat for 1 hour or until soft and easily pierced by a fork. Remove from pot and cool. Cut in half and remove all the seeds or they will make the cake very bitter. Finely mince in food processor.

Grind almonds with ½ cup sugar in a clean and dry food processor until fine. Transfer to a large bowl and add remaining sugar and orange pulp. Blend in yolks.

Beat egg whites until stiff and fold into cake batter. Pour batter into pan and bake for 1 hour or until cake is light brown on top and feels firm.

Cool on rack for about 20 minutes and then remove rim and cool completely. Dust with confectioners' sugar if desired.

Yield: 8–10 servings

IRISH CREAM BUNDT CAKE

Butter and flour for pan
1 cup chopped pecans
1 18-ounce package yellow cake mix
1 ¾-ounce package instant vanilla pudding mix
4 large eggs
¼ cup water
½ cup vegetable oil
¾ cup Irish Cream liqueur

Preheat oven to 325°.

Butter and flour a 10" bundt pan. Sprinkle chopped nuts evenly over bottom of pan.

In a large bowl, combine cake mix and pudding mix. Mix in eggs, water, oil and liqueur. Beat for 5 minutes on high. Pour batter over nuts.

Bake 60 minutes or until done. Cool 10 minutes, then invert onto serving dish. Prick top and sides of cake with fork. Spoon glaze over top and brush into sides.

Glaze:
½ cup butter
1 cup granulated sugar
¾ cup water
¼ cup Irish Cream liqueur

Combine butter, water and sugar in pan. Bring to a boil. Simmer for 5 minutes, stirring constantly. Remove from heat and add liqueur.

Yield: 10–12 servings

"When my grandmother became ill and nursing care started, she no longer traveled to Michigan. That's when my overnights or weekends at the house began. We ate dinner on trays in her room, and my favorite dessert was broiled grapefruit with a little brown sugar on top. Being alone with my grandmother was one of my favorite times with her."

—MARGARET GAMBLE MESSLER WINSLOW

LEMON WALNUT BARS

Crust:
½ cup butter, softened, plus extra for pan
½ cup granulated sugar
1 tablespoon grated lemon zest
1¼ cups all-purpose flour

Preheat oven to 350°. Grease a 9" x 13" cake pan or baking dish.

Beat butter, sugar, and lemon zest with a mixer or by hand until creamy. Gradually mix in flour to form a soft, crumbly dough. Press evenly into a prepared pan.

Bake until golden around the edges, 10–12 minutes.

Filling:

2 eggs
1 cup packed brown sugar
¼ cup all-purpose flour
¼ teaspoon baking powder
1 teaspoon grated lemon zest
1 cup finely chopped walnuts

In a bowl whisk eggs, brown sugar, baking powder, and lemon zest. Stir in walnuts. Spread evenly over the baked crust.

Return to oven and bake until golden, 15–20 minutes.

Lemon Glaze:
1 tablespoon butter, softened
1 cup powdered sugar, sifted
2 tablespoons freshly squeezed lemon juice

Beat butter, sugar, and lemon juice until smooth. Spread evenly over hot filling, just after it has been removed from the oven.

Let cool completely in the pan on a rack. Cut into bars or squares.

Yield: 24 squares (6 rows x 4 rows) or 32 bars (8 rows x 4 rows)

DELICIOUS, YUMMY BROWNIES

½ pound butter, plus extra for pan
½ pound bittersweet chocolate
4 large eggs
½ teaspoon salt
1 cup sugar
1 cup brown sugar
1 cup flour
1–2 cups chopped nuts, optional

Preheat oven to 350°.

Melt butter and chocolate in double boiler.

Beat eggs and add the salt and sugars. Stir into the butter-chocolate mixture and add flour. Add the nuts, if desired.

Pour into buttered 9" x 13" pan.

Bake for 45 minutes.

Yield: 16–20 pieces

GERMAN APPLE CAKE

6 apples, peeled and cored
3 cups sugar
3 large eggs, unbeaten
3 teaspoons vanilla
¾ cup oil, plus extra for pan
3 cups flour, sifted
3 teaspoons cinnamon
3 teaspoons baking soda
1½ teaspoons salt
1½ cups chopped walnuts

Preheat oven to 350°.

Cut each apple into 16 slices. Add flour and then add the other ingredients, except nuts, to apples. Mix well. Add nuts and mix again. Bake in 9" x 13" greased pan for 1½ hours. Cool and frost, or omit frosting and serve with lightly sweetened whipped cream.

Frosting:
½ cup butter or margarine, softened
3 ounces cream cheese
1 teaspoon vanilla
1 cup powdered sugar

Mix all ingredients with beater until fluffy.

Yield: 12–16 servings

FORGOTTEN COOKIES

2 large egg whites
⅔ cup sugar
Pinch of salt
1 cup chopped nuts
1 cup chocolate chips
1 teaspoon vanilla

Preheat oven to 350°.

Beat egg whites until foamy. Gradually add sugar and continue beating until stiff. Add remaining ingredients and mix well.

Drop cookies by teaspoonfuls onto ungreased foil. Place cookies in oven and immediately turn oven off. Leave in oven 8 hours or overnight.

Yield: 30–36 cookies

NANA'S APRICOT BARS

½ pound dried apricots, chopped
¾ cup sugar
¾ cup water
½ teaspoon lemon or orange zest, optional
2 teaspoons lemon juice
1¼ cups oatmeal
1¼ cups flour
1 cup brown sugar, packed
1 teaspoon baking soda
4 ounces unsalted butter, melted, plus extra for pan

Preheat oven to 325°.

Mix apricots, sugar, water, zest and lemon juice in a heavy saucepan. Bring to a boil, then simmer for 5–10 minutes until syrupy. Stir occasionally. Cool.

Mix oatmeal, flour, sugar and baking soda until well blended. Stir in the melted butter and mix well.

Pat ⅔ of the mixture into a lightly greased 9" x 13" pan. Press firmly and evenly in place. Spread the apricot mixture evenly on top of the mixture. Top with remaining oat mixture. Press down lightly.

Bake for 30–40 minutes until lightly browned. Cool and cut into squares.

Yield: 16–20 bars

"A special treat for Dyke and me was helping my grandmother with the saccharin in her tea. Each week, one of us was allowed to get up from our seat, take two little pills out of a tiny enamel pill box with an attached lid, which was always next to her tea cup, put them into her tea, and watch them dissolve."
—MARGARET GAMBLE MESSLER WINSLOW

CHOCOLATE CHUNK OATMEAL COCONUT COOKIES

2 sticks (1 cup) unsalted butter, softened, plus extra for cookie sheets
1 cup packed brown sugar
6 tablespoons granulated sugar
2 large eggs
1½ teaspoons vanilla
½ teaspoon baking soda
½ teaspoon salt
1 cup all-purpose flour
2¼ cups old-fashioned oats
1½ cups packed finely shredded unsweetened coconut
12 ounces semisweet or bittersweet packaged chocolate chunks
¾ cup almonds with skins (4 ounces), toasted

Preheat oven to 375°.

Beat together butter and sugars in a bowl with an electric mixer at high speed until fluffy. Add eggs and beat until just blended. Beat in vanilla, baking soda and salt. Add flour and mix at low speed until just blended. Stir in oats, coconut, chocolate and almonds.

Arrange ¼ cup mounds of cookie dough about 3 apart on 2 lightly buttered large baking sheets (about 8 cookies per sheet), then gently pat down each mound to about ½" thick. Bake in upper and lower thirds of oven, switching position and rotating pans halfway through baking, until golden, 15–18 minutes total.

Cool cookies on sheets 1 minute. Transfer with a spatula to racks to cool completely.

Repeat until batter is finished.

Yield: 20–24 large cookies

CRANBERRY NOEL COOKIES

2 sticks unsalted butter at room temperature
½ cup sugar
2 tablespoons milk
1 teaspoon vanilla extract
2½ cups sifted flour
½ teaspoon salt
¾ cup dried cranberries
½ cup chopped pecans
Unsweetened shredded coconut

Preheat oven to 375°.

With electric mixer, beat butter until fluffy. Add sugar and beat for 2 minutes. Add milk and vanilla. Sift together flour and salt and gradually add to butter mixture scraping down the bowl while mixing.

Remove from mixer; fold in cranberries and pecans. Form dough into two logs 1½" in diameter. Brush logs with water and roll in coconut.

Wrap each log in plastic wrap and chill in refrigerator at least 2 hours or overnight.

Slice chilled rolls ¼" thick. Bake on Silpat™ or parchment paper-lined baking sheet for 10–12 minutes until edges are golden. Cool on rack.

Yield: 4–5 dozen cookies

PAT'S CANDIED NUTS

2 egg whites
1½ tablespoons water
1 teaspoon vanilla extract
1 pound raw pecan halves
1 pound raw almonds, whole
1 pound raw cashews, whole
1 pound raw walnut halves
1¼ cups sugar
2 teaspoons cinnamon
1 tablespoon kosher salt
½ teaspoon nutmeg

Preheat oven to 325°.

In a very large 5–quart bowl or pan, beat the egg whites, water and vanilla extract until very frothy and foamy. Add all the nuts and mix until the nuts are damp. Stir and mix thoroughly. Mix together, sugar, cinnamon, salt and nutmeg and add to the nuts, stirring until the nuts are well coated.

Spray 2 large jelly roll pans with Pam® or cooking spray. Spread the nuts onto them.

Bake for 1 hour. Turn and mix the nuts every 15 minutes. Be especially watchful the last 15 minutes to prevent the nuts from burning.

Cool nuts in the pan. Store in airtight containers.

Yield: About 10 cups

Note: Use raw nuts only.

LEMON ZEST COOKIES

1 cup unsalted butter
1 cup sugar, plus a little more for sprinkling
2 cups flour
Grated zest of one lemon
1 tablespoon lemon juice

Preheat oven to 350°.

Cream together butter, sugar, lemon zest and juice.

Add flour gradually and knead, adding flour as necessary, until dough no longer sticks to your fingers.

Take a pinch of dough and roll it into a ball the size of a small walnut.

Drop onto a cookie sheet and press the ball flat (about $\frac{1}{8}$" thick) with the bottom of a glass dipped in sugar. Continue with the rest of the dough, leaving about 1"–2" between cookies.

Sprinkle with additional sugar if desired.

Bake until barely browned at the edges, about 10 minutes. Remove from oven and transfer to racks to cool.

Yield: 30–36 cookies

MAPLE PECAN COOKIES

2 sticks butter, softened
½ cup granulated white sugar
1 large egg yolk
3 tablespoons pure maple syrup
½ teaspoon vanilla extract
2 cups all-purpose flour
1½ cups coarsely chopped pecans, optional

In a medium bowl, beat the butter until pale, about 2 minutes. Gradually beat in sugar until well blended. Add maple syrup, egg yolk and vanilla. Stir in flour and add pecans. Mix until well blended.

Divide dough in half (floured hands are helpful) and form into 2 logs (about 1½" in diameter) and wrap each in plastic wrap. Refrigerate until firm, at least 2 hours or overnight.

Preheat oven to 350°.

Remove one log from the refrigerator and cut into ½" thick slices. Repeat with the remaining log. Place slices on an ungreased cookie sheet and bake 20–25 minutes until golden.

Transfer to a wire rack to cool. Can be stored in an airtight container for 1 week.

Yield: 3–4 dozen cookies

ALMOND TORTONI

1 egg white
Dash of cream of tartar
Pinch of salt
⅓ cup sugar
1 cup heavy cream
1 tablespoon almond extract
Slivered almonds

Using a mixer or whisk, beat the egg white with cream of tartar and salt until frothy. Continue to beat, gradually adding 2 tablespoons of sugar, until stiff peaks form.

Using clean beaters, whip the cream with the remaining sugar until stiff. Add extract to the cream and fold the whipped cream into the stiff egg white. Spoon mixture into crinkle cups or paper cupcake liners set in muffin pans. Sprinkle with slivered almonds and freeze.

Yield: 8 servings

ALMOND WALNUT TOFFEE

1 cup butter, plus more for pan
2½ cups sugar
1½ cups almonds, sliced or chopped
1 teaspoon vanilla
1 pound semi-sweet chocolate
1 cup walnuts, finely chopped

Melt butter in a heavy saucepan over low heat. Stir in sugar and cook until mixture comes to a boil. Remove from heat and stir in almonds. Cook over moderately high heat without stirring until a candy thermometer registers 290°.

Remove from heat and add vanilla. Pour into a buttered 12" x 18" jelly roll pan. Cool completely.

Melt chocolate in double boiler over low heat. Spread half over the top of the candy. Dust with walnuts. Chill until set.

Invert candy onto a piece of waxed paper. Spread toffee with remaining chocolate and dust with remaining nuts. When set, break into pieces and store in an airtight container.

Yield: 3 pounds

LEMON PEEL SHERBET

2 cups milk
1½ cups sugar
Juice of 3-4 lemons
Grated zest of 2 lemons
2 egg whites
1 cup whipping cream

Combine milk, sugar, lemon juice and zest and mix well. Pour into ice tray and freeze about 1 hour, or until mushy. Beat the egg whites until barely stiff. In a separate bowl, beat the cream until it is custard-like. Fold these two together and add to the lemon mixture. Freeze for 2½–3 hours. Sherbet is best if it is not too hard.

Yield: 6–8 servings

MAXINE'S FUDGE SQUARES

½ cup butter
3 squares bittersweet chocolate or 8 tablespoons cocoa
2 large eggs
1 cup sugar
½ cup flour
½ cup nuts
Dash of salt
1 teaspoon vanilla

Preheat oven to 375°.

Melt butter with chocolate over low heat. In a separate bowl, beat eggs and add the sugar, beating it well. Combine the 2 mixtures and sift in flour. Add nuts, salt, and vanilla.

Pour into either an 8" x 8" pan or 9" x 9" pan.

Bake for 20–25 minutes.

Yield: 16 pieces

CELEBRITY MOCHA FREEZE

1 pint whipping cream
⅓ cup brandy
⅔ cup chocolate syrup
1 quart coffee ice cream, softened
6 ounces semi-sweet chocolate morsels
¾ cup almonds, chopped and toasted
Whipped cream and chocolate sprinkles for garnish

In a large bowl, mix whipping cream, brandy and chocolate syrup. Beat until thickened, but not stiff. Fold in ice cream, chocolate chips and almonds.

Freeze uncovered until solid on top, but still soft inside, about 1 hour. Remove from freezer. Stir well to bring chips and almonds from the bottom of the bowl. Cover and freeze until solid. Mixture will keep in freezer for several months.

To serve, spoon frozen mixture into individual serving dishes and garnish with whipped cream and chocolate sprinkles.

Yield: 8–10 servings

FROZEN MYSTERY

½ gallon rich vanilla ice cream
5 ounces apricot preserves
3 ounces frozen lemonade concentrate, thawed

Soften the ice cream and add preserves and lemonade. Mix all together in a decorative serving bowl and return to the freezer for at least 3 hours.

Yield: 12 servings

PUMPKIN MOUSSE ICE CREAM PIE WITH CARAMEL SAUCE

1½ cups crushed gingersnap cookies
⅓ cup melted butter or margarine
1 pint vanilla ice cream
1 cup canned pumpkin
¾ cup sugar
1½ teaspoons pumpkin pie spice
1 cup whipping cream
½ teaspoon vanilla
Sauce

Preheat oven to 350°.

Combine crushed gingersnaps and butter. Press onto bottom and sides of a 9" pie plate. Bake for 15 minutes. Cool.

Soften ice cream. Spread over gingersnap crust. Freeze.

Combine pumpkin, sugar and pumpkin pie spice. Beat whipping cream and vanilla until stiff. Fold into pumpkin mixture. Spread and mound over ice cream. Freeze.

Serve with caramel sauce.

Sauce:
1 12¼-ounce jar caramel or butterscotch sauce
½ cup canned pumpkin
½ teaspoon pumpkin pie spice

Combine sauce, pumpkin, and pumpkin pie spice. Heat if desired.

Yield: 6–8 servings

INDEX

PHOTOGRAPHY CREDITS

FRONT COVER Meg McComb
*Three-panel embroidered screen
and chair from Gustav Stickley's
Craftsman Workshops, circa 1909,
upstairs guest room*

FRONTISPIECE Tim Street-Porter
*Detail of sideboard with art glass
windows designed by Greene and
Greene, dining room*

PAGE 7 *Charles Sumner Greene
and Henry Mather Greene
photographs, courtesy of the
Los Angeles Public Library*

PAGE 12 Tim Street-Porter
Kitchen and porch detail

PAGE 14 Tim Street-Porter
*Entry hall with art glass door
and living room detail with piano
and bench*

PAGE 16 Tim Street-Porter
Dining room

PAGE 31 Meg McComb
*Mary Gamble's journal with
Rookwood vase, Mary and David
Gamble's bedroom*

PAGE 41 Meg McComb
Detail of window seat, upstairs hall

PAGE 53 Meg McComb
*Detail of dressing table, first floor
guest room*

PAGE 65 Meg McComb
Detail of writing desk, living room

PAGE 79 Meg McComb
*Detail of table and chair on Aunt
Julia's sleeping porch with photo of
Aunt Julia, circa 1915*

PAGE 89 Meg McComb
*Wooden bowl and chopper, carved
by Charles Greene for his family*

PAGE 119 Meg McComb
*Detail of cabinet with Tiffany
Studios stemware, dining room*

PAGE 131 Meg McComb
Detail of kitchen table and cabinet

BACK COVER Alex Vertikoff
The Gamble House

Gamble family photos and Mary Gamble's recipes, courtesy of the Gamble family collection

TOQUES OFF TO OUR PATRONS

Anonymous (7)

Grace Anderson

John Azar

Marcia Bell

LaVonne Bennett

Cheryl Bode &
    Robin Colman

Thelma Borman

Ted, Will & Julia Bosley

Perry Botkin &
    Liza Hennessy Botkin

Janet Boyer

Liz Corey Braislin

Kori Capaldi

Sandy Chapman

Carolyn Chenoweth

Corinna Cotsen &
    Lee Rosenbaum

Jean Crawford

Barbara & Ivan Cury

Audel and Lynne Davis

Judith Dawson

Docent Class of 1988

Sarah Gamble Epstein

Jetty Fong

Sidney Gally in memory of
    Helen Gally

Steffanie & Geoffrey Gee

Buff Gontier

Joan Graham

Douglas & Barbara Hadsell

Doreen Hagan

Denise & Donald Hahn

Elizabeth & Robert Harris

Peggy L. Hayek

Patty J. Heather

Glenice Hershberger

Tracy G. Hirrel

Jan Horner

Elizabeth Humble

Ann Hyatt

Helga Johnstone

Mary Jones

Joan Lange Kaas

Sylvia L. Kahrl

Nancy Kailey

Cindy Kalter

Ellen & Harvey Knell

Ralph & Mary Knowles

Sheila Larson & Family

Randy and Anne Leach

Pat Lem

Paula Sigman Lowery

Joann Lynch

Randell L. Makinson

Virginia M. Martens

Eleanor Portilla Maynard

Joseph D. Messler, Jr.

Kennon Miedema

Duane Miller & JP Sabarots

Hilda Opel Nichols

Florence Valentine Omens

Bret Parsons

Mrs. George E. Parsons, Jr.

Evelyn & Charles Plemons

Victor Regnier

Elizabeth A. Rodeno

Millie Rodstrom

Cleo Rogers

Carole Rose

Kathy Russell

Patricia Savoie

Kaye Sergeant

Poppy Solomon

Winnie Staniford

Jack Stumpf

Sally Swan

Doug & Beth Swift

Timothy Toohey

Brookes Treidler

Mary D. Tumilty

Diana Vlacich

Jocelyn Cady Vortmann

Sylvia Watson

Mrs. Ted Will

Margaret M. Winslow

Sue Zanteson

Isabelle Zimmerman

In memory of
    Mary Alice Stumpf

*Thanks to those whose
support arrived after the
book went to press.*

ACKNOWLEDGEMENTS

In 2006, a small cadre of docents proposed a new cookbook to honor the centennial year of The Gamble House in 2008. The idea attracted many docents who submitted recipes to the quickly formed Cookbook Committee. It was a non-stop process carried out with diligence, perseverance, and affection.

We are indebted to the docents who volunteered time to share, review, and select recipes, incorporating several recipes published in prior collections and to the docents who tested (and tasted) recipes, typed drafts, copyedited, and proofread.

To The Gamble House staff — especially Ted Bosley, Anne Malleck, Robina Mapstone, Ann Scheid, Sarah Smith, Cynthia Batterson-Rice, Judith Benda, Kori Capaldi, and Everardo Farias — we offer our profound thanks for the generous amount of time, guidance and white-gloved assistance donated to this project. Thanks to Leslie Baker, Ann Gray, Peter Shamray, and Suellen Martensson for patiently and delicately educating us about the publishing process.

Our infinite gratitude to Terry Gamble Boyer, Margaret Gamble Messler Winslow, Joseph D. Messler, Jr., Tracy Gamble Hirrell, Jane McElroy, Mark Peel, Meg McComb, Robert S. Harris, James O. Cury, Dottie O'Carroll, Lee Rosenbaum, Paula L. Woods, Martha Casselman, Nadia Farida, Felix Liddell, Ivan Cury, and to the Docent Council Board of Directors.

Finally, our appreciation to all of you who share the love and enthusiasm for The Gamble House and who encouraged us by your participation, financial support, and energy to make this book a reality.

The Cookbook Committee

CONTRIBUTORS

Edward R. Bosley

Edward R. Bosley has been director of The Gamble House since 1992 and is a renowned authority on architects Charles Sumner Greene and Henry Mather Greene and the American Arts and Crafts movement. He is the author of "Greene & Greene" (Phaidon, 2000) and co-editor of "A 'New and Native' Beauty: The Art and Craft of Greene & Greene" (Merrell, 2008).

Robert S. Harris

Robert S. Harris is a former Dean of the School of Architecture at the University of Southern California (USC), as well as a former Director of USC Graduate Studies in Architecture. One of the first five educators in the U.S. named Distinguished Professor by the Association of Collegiate Schools of Architecture, Professor Harris has won design and research awards for work in Oregon and California. He served as Chairman of the Los Angeles Mayor's Design Advisory Panel and of the Downtown Strategic Plan Advisory Committee. He was founder and past president of the Urban Design Advisory Coalition and a former president of the Los Angeles Conservancy.

Meg McComb

Photographer Meg McComb, formerly a restauranteur, chef, and food stylist, began providing hand-tipped photocards to her culinary friends in the 1990s. Her attention to detail, visual ingenuity, and an eye for composition combine harmoniously with her travels abroad and at home. The resulting photography has received national acclaim.

Mark Peel

Mark Peel is the Executive Chef and owner of Campanile and co-founded La Brea Bakery. In 2001 Campanile received the prestigious James Beard Award for Outstanding Restaurant in the U.S. In his early career he worked with Wolfgang Puck, Alice Waters, and Jonathon Waxman. Peel has co-authored two cookbooks with Nancy Silverton, "Two Chefs Cook for Family and Friends (Warner Books), and "The Food of Campanile" (Villard). He is currently working on a new cookbook.